M000249404

Differentiating Instruction With Menus

for the Inclusive Classroom

Language Arts

Differentiating Instruction With Menus

for the Inclusive Classroom

Language Arts

Laurie E. Westphal

PRUFROCK PRESS INC.
WACO, TEXAS

Library of Congress Cataloging-in-Publication Data

Westphal, Laurie E., 1967-
 Differentiating instruction with menus for the inclusive classroom. Language arts, grades K-2 / by Laurie E. Westphal.
    pages cm
 Includes bibliographical references.
 ISBN 978-1-61821-034-0 (pbk.)
 1. Language arts (Elementary) 2. Individualized instruction. 3. Inclusive education. 4. Mixed ability grouping in education. I. Title.
 LB1576.W48459 2013
 372.6--dc23
                        2012039529

Edited by Jennifer Robins

Production design by Raquel Trevino

ISBN-13: 978-1-61821-034-0

At the time of this book's publication, all facts and figures cited are the most current available; all telephone numbers, addresses, and website URLs are accurate and active; all publications, organizations, websites, and other resources exist as described in this book; and all have been verified. The author and Prufrock Press make no warranty or guarantee concerning the information and materials given out by organizations or content found at websites, and we are not responsible for any changes that occur after this book's publication. If you find an error or believe that a resource listed here is not as described, please contact Prufrock Press.

Prufrock Press Inc.
P.O. Box 8813
Waco, TX 76714-8813
Phone: (800) 998-2208
Fax: (800) 240-0333
http://www.prufrock.com

CONTENTS

Author's Note

If you are familiar with books on various differentiation strategies, then you probably know about my Differentiating Instruction With Menus series, and you may be wondering about the differences between that series and this one, the Differentiating Instruction With Menus for the Inclusive Classroom series. In fact, when we first discussed creating this series, my editor asked how we could avoid having one series "cannibalize" (graphic, but a great word!) the other. Well, here is how I envision the two series being used:

These two series stand on their own if:
- You teach mostly lower ability, on-level, and ESL students and would like to modify your lessons on your own to accommodate a few advanced students. In this case, use this series, Differentiating Instruction With Menus for the Inclusive Classroom.
- You teach mostly advanced and high-ability students and would like to modify your lessons on your own to accommodate a few lower level students. In this case, use the Differentiating Instruction With Menus series.

These two series can serve as companions to one another if:
- You teach students with a wide range of abilities (from special education to gifted) and would benefit from having a total of three menus for a given topic of study: those for lower ability and on-level students (provided by this series, Differentiating Instruction With Menus for the Inclusive Classroom) and those for high-ability students (provided by the Differentiating Instruction With Menus series).

The menu designs used in this book reflect a successful modification technique I began using in my own classroom as the range of my students' ability levels widened. I experimented with many ways to use menus, from having students of all ability levels work on the same menu with the same expectations, to having everyone work on the same menu with modified contracted expectations, to using leveled menus where each student received one of three menus with some overlapping activities based on readiness, abilities, or preassessment results. I found that if the students in a given classroom had similar ability levels, I could use one menu with every student with slight modifications; however, the greater the span of ability levels, the more I needed the different leveled menus to reach everyone. Each book in the Differentiating Instruction With Menus for the Inclusive Classroom series has two leveled menus for the objectives covered: a lower level menu indicated by a ▲ and an on-level menu indicated by a ●. This way, teachers can provide more options to students with diverse abilities in the inclusive classroom. If used with the corresponding book in the Differentiating Instruction With Menus series, the teacher has a total of three leveled menus to work with.

Many teachers have told me how helpful the original Differentiating Instruction With Menus books are and how they have modified the books' menus to meet the needs of their lower level students. Teachers are always the first to make adjustments and find solutions, but wouldn't it be great if they had these preparations and changes already made for them? This is the purpose of the Differentiating Instruction With Menus for the Inclusive Classroom series.

—Laurie E. Westphal

CHAPTER 1

Choice in the Inclusive Primary Classroom

"So, I can do as many as I want? Really?" stuttered one of my second-grade students as he looked, surprised, from the paper in his hand to me. I had just handed out a Getting to Know You Pick 3 menu and explained to the small-group members that they would need to complete at least three choices from the list in order to share a few things about themselves with the group and me.

Let's begin by addressing the concept of the inclusive classroom. The term *inclusive* (vs. exclusive) leads one to believe that we are discussing a situation in which all students are included. In the simplest of terms, that is exactly what we are referring to as an inclusive classroom: a classroom that may have special needs students, on-level students, bilingual or ESL students, and gifted students. Although the concept is a simple one, the considerations are significant.

When thinking about the inclusive classroom and its unique ambiance, one must first consider the needs of the range of students within the classroom. Mercer, Lane, Jordan, Allsopp, and Eisele (1996) stated it best in their assessment of the needs in an inclusive classroom:

> Students who are academically gifted, those who have had abundant experiences, and those who have demonstrated

proficiency with lesson content typically tend to perform well when instruction is anchored at the "implicit" end of the instructional continuum. In contrast, low-performing students (i.e., students at risk for school failure, students with learning disabilities, and students with other special needs) and students with limited experience or proficiency with lesson content are most successful when instruction is explicit. Students with average academic performance tend to benefit most from the use of a variety of instructional methods that address individual needs. Instructional decisions for most students, therefore, should be based on assessment of individual needs. (pp. 230–231)

Acknowledging these varied and often contradictory needs that arise within an inclusive classroom can lead to frustration when trying to make one assignment or task fit everyone's needs. There are few—if any—traditional, teacher-directed lessons that can be implicit, explicit, and based on individual needs all at the same time. There is, however, one technique that tries to accomplish this: choice.

CHOICE: THE SUPERMAN OF TECHNIQUES?

Can the offering of appropriate choices really be the hero of the inclusive classroom? Can it leap buildings in a single bound and meet the needs of our implicit, explicit, and individual interests? Yes! By considering the use and benefits of choice, we can see that by offering choices, teachers really can meet the needs of the whole range of students in a primary inclusive classroom. Ask adults whether they would prefer to choose what to do or be told what to do, and of course, they will say they would prefer to have a choice. Students have the same feelings. Although they may not be experienced in making choices, they will make choices based on their needs, just as adults do—which makes everyone involved in the inclusive experience a little less stressed and frustrated.

PRIMARY STUDENTS AND CHOICE

"I think it is the best one because I like it."

—Kindergarten student, when asked to defend his activity of choice

Choice can be frustrating for both the teacher (who is trying to draw the best from his or her young students) and the students (who are trying to do what the teacher is asking, but are just not sure how to do it). Choice and independent thinking on a higher level are developmental in nature, as well as cognitive skills. When given a choice between tools to complete a product, most primary students have not yet developed their higher level thinking skills enough to respond with a well-thought-out, analytical response. Instead, a 5-year-old may defend or evaluate his choice by stating that it was the one he liked or that it was red, his favorite color. Does that imply that primary students are not capable of making choices or processing at the analysis level or higher? Definitely not! Primary students are very capable of making choices and enjoy doing so with some guidance. This guidance comes in minimizing the number of choices a student faces at once, as well as assisting in the choice process.

MAKING GOOD CHOICES IS A SKILL

"I wanted you to know, I never thought of [making good choices as a skill] that way. That really opened my eyes."

—Kindergarten teacher

When we think of making good choices as a skill, much like writing an effective paragraph, it becomes easy enough to understand the processes needed to encourage primary students to make their own choices. In keeping with this analogy, children could certainly figure out how to write on their own, perhaps even how to compose sentences and paragraphs by using other examples as models. Imagine, however, the progress and strength of the writing produced when children are given guidance and even the most basic of instruction on how to accomplish this task. The written piece is still their own, but the quality of the finished piece is much stronger when guidance is given during the process. The same is true with the quality of choices children can make in the classroom.

As with writing, students—especially those with special needs—can make choices on their own, but when the teacher provides background knowledge and assistance, those choices become more meaningful, and the products become richer. Although all students certainly need guidance, primary students will need the most; they often have not been in an educational setting long enough to have experienced different products, and the idea of choice is usually new to them. Some children may have experienced choice only when their parents allowed them to choose between different outfits or breakfast options for the day. Some may not have experienced even this level of choice. This can cause frustration for both the teacher and the student.

TEACHING CHOICES AS A SKILL

"When it comes to choice, some of my students just aren't receptive."

—First-grade teacher

So, what is the best way to provide this guidance and develop students' skill of making good choices? First, choose the appropriate number of options for your students. Although the goal might be to have students choose between nine different options, teachers should start by having their students choose between three predetermined choices the first day (if they were using a Three-Shape menu, students might choose one circle activity from the row of three circles). Then, after those products have been created, students can choose between another set of three options a few days later and perhaps another three the following week. By breaking down students' choices, teachers are reinforcing how to approach a more complex and/or varied choice format in the future. Primary students— even kindergarten students—can work up to making complex choices from longer lists of options as their choice skill level increases.

"My first menu bombed. I had given it out to the students, told them to pick what they wanted to do, [and given them] the deadline at the end of the week. Students either bugged me all week with questions or they didn't do anything. . . . The second one went so much better. I did a build-up with lots of excitement and guidance for each choice. My students did a great job! Some even did more than the minimum!"

—Second-grade teacher

Second, students will need guidance on how to select the options that are right for them. They may not automatically gravitate toward options without an exciting and detailed description of each choice. For the most part, primary students are still in the "pleasing the teacher" phase, which means that when given a choice, they will usually choose what they think will make the teacher happy. This means that when the teacher discusses the different menu options, the teacher has to be equally as excited about all of them. The discussion of the different choices has to be animated and specific. For example, if the content is all very similar, the focus would be on the product: "If you want to do some singing, this one is for you!" or "If you want to write and draw, circle this one as a maybe!" Sometimes, choices may differ based on both content and product, in which case both can be pointed out to students to assist them in making good choices for themselves: "You have some different choices in our Earth science unit. If you want to do something with dinosaurs and drawing, circle this one as a maybe. If you are thinking you want to do something with collecting rocks, this one might be for you." Primary students, although egocentric in nature, have not yet pondered who they really are and often have trouble choosing between product types and content on their own. The more exposure they have to the think-aloud process through teacher demonstration, the more skillful they become in making their own choices.

WHY IS CHOICE IMPORTANT?

"I liked making the board game. Can I make one for my next menu, too?"

—Second-grade student

One benefit of choice is its ability to meet the needs of so many different students and their learning styles. Teachers are aware that their students have different learning styles and understand the importance of accommodating different learning preferences in their classroom. In order to make this more feasible for teachers, the integration of choice can allow students to experience opportunities to find their niche. Unlike older elementary students, primary students have not been engaged in the learning process long enough to recognize their own strengths and weaknesses, as well as their preferred ways of learning; therefore, they need to be exposed to multiple options so they can begin to discover their preferences. By allowing choice, students are better able to narrow their options in the future and choose what best fits their learning preferences and educational needs.

Another benefit of choice is a greater sense of independence for the students. What a powerful feeling! This independence looks different at each grade level in the primary grades. It may be a kindergarten child working independently for an extended period time on a product he has selected or a second grader with special needs reading about a topic she has selected based on her interest. Once students understand that the goal is to produce *their* version of a task, that they will have the opportunity to design and create a product based on what they envision—they will really want to create something of their own. They will, however, still need some guidance and reassurance that their approach to a task is on the right track, so as teachers we are not out of a job by incorporating choice! The independence that structured choice at this level fosters simply allows us more time to facilitate and guide students in the direction they have selected for themselves. Allowing all of our students to show their learning by choosing the products they create helps develop independence at an early age at any ability level.

> *"I like getting to pick what I want."*
>
> —First-grade student

Strengthened student focus on the required content is a third benefit of choice. When students have choices in the activities they wish to complete, they are more focused on the learning that leads to their chosen product. Students become excited when they learn information that can help them develop a product they would like to create. Students will pay close attention to instruction and have an immediate application for the knowledge being presented in class. Also, if students are focused, they are less likely to be off task during instruction.

The final benefit (although I am sure there are many more) is the simple fact that by offering varied choices at appropriate levels, you can address implicit instructional options, explicit instructional options, and individual needs without anyone getting overly frustrated or overworked. There are few teaching strategies that can meet all of these different needs at once—it boils down to making the experience more personal for all of our students, and choice can do this.

Many a great educator has referred to the idea that the best learning takes place when students have a desire to learn and can feel successful while doing it. The majority of our primary students come to school with open minds, wanting to fill them with knowledge that is valuable and meaningful. By incorporating different activities from which to choose, students stretch beyond what they already know, and teachers create a void that needs to be filled. This void leads to a desire to learn.

HOW CAN PRIMARY TEACHERS PROVIDE CHOICES?

"I was pretty skeptical about using a menu with my [kids with special needs] since they need so many modifications, but I found that by using mainly graphics and cutting the menu like you suggested it was easy for them to grasp."

—First-grade teacher

When people go to a restaurant, the common goal is to find something on the menu to satisfy their hunger. Students come into our classrooms having a hunger as well—a hunger for learning. Choice menus are a way of allowing our students to choose how they would like to satisfy that hunger. At the very least, a menu is a list of choices that students use to choose an activity (or activities) they would like to complete to show what they have learned. At best, it is a complex system in which students earn points by making choices from different areas of study. Depending on the experience and comfort level of the students, the menus can also incorporate a free-choice option for those "picky eaters" who would like to place a special order to satisfy their learning hunger.

The next few sections provide examples of the types of menus that will be used in this book: target-based menus, in which students have a goal set by the design of the menu, and point-based menus, in which students select a product to reach a point goal. Each menu has its own benefits, limitations or drawbacks, and time considerations. An explanation of the free-choice option and its management will follow the information on each type of menu.

THREE-SHAPE MENU

"This was the easiest menu for me to modify for my students. Being able to cut it into pieces for those who needed less choice was a super easy modification!"

—Second-grade teacher

Description

The Three-Shape menu (see Figure 1) is a target-based menu with a total of nine predetermined choices for students. The choices are created at the various levels of Bloom's revised taxonomy (Anderson & Krathwohl, 2001) and incorporate different learning styles. All products carry the same weight for grading and have similar expectations for completion time and effort.

Benefits

Ease of modification. This menu can easily be modified by simply cutting the menu into strips of the same shape. As students complete a choice, they are given another strip of shapes. The choice

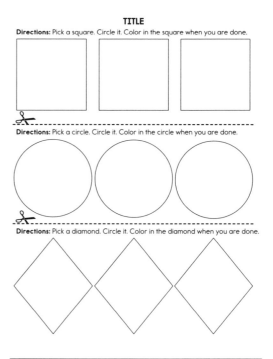

TITLE

Directions: Pick a square. Circle it. Color in the square when you are done.

Directions: Pick a circle. Circle it. Color in the circle when you are done.

Directions: Pick a diamond. Circle it. Color in the diamond when you are done.

Figure 1. Three-Shape menu example.

then becomes one of three options, rather than three of nine, a much more daunting option.

Flexibility. This menu can cover either one topic in depth or three different objectives. When this menu covers just one objective, students have the option of completing three products: one from each shape group.

Friendly design. Students quickly understand how to use this menu. It is easy to explain how to make the choices based on the various shapes, and the shapes can be used to visually separate expectations (e.g., squares one day, circles the next).

Weighting. All products are equally weighted, so recording grades and maintaining paperwork are easily accomplished with this menu.

Short time period. This menu is intended for shorter periods of time, from one day to one week in the primary classroom.

Limitations

Few topics. This menu covers one or three topics.

Time Considerations

This menu usually is intended for shorter periods of completion time— at most, it should take one week in a primary inclusive classroom. If the menu focuses on one topic in depth, it can be completed in 1–2 days.

MEAL MENU

"Can I have dinner first?"

—Second-grade student with special needs in an inclusive classroom

Description

The Meal menu (see Figure 2) is a target-based menu with a total of at least nine predetermined choices as well as at least one enrichment option for students. The choices are created at the various levels of Bloom's revised taxonomy and incorporate different learning styles. All products carry the same weight for grading and have similar expectations for completion time and effort. The enrichment options can be used for extra credit or replace another meal option at the teacher's discretion.

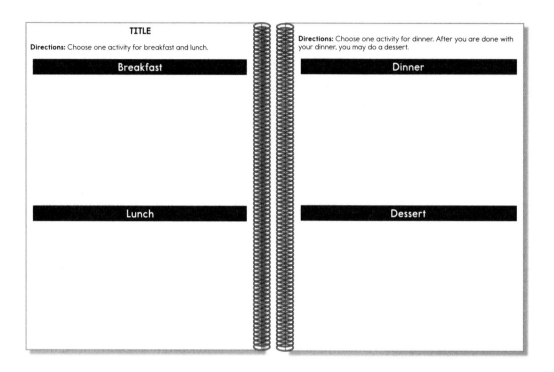

Figure 2. Meal menu example.

Benefits

Ease of modification. This menu can easily be modified by simply cutting the menu in half along its "spiral." Students first receive their breakfast and lunch choices; once completed, the teacher will provide the dinner and enriching dessert option. The choice can become one of six options, rather than 10 at once.

Flexibility. This menu can cover either one topic in depth or three different objectives. When this menu covers just one objective, students have the option of completing three products from different levels of Bloom's revised taxonomy: one for each meal.

Friendly design. Students quickly understand how to use this menu because of its real-world application.

Weighting. All products are equally weighted, so recording grades and maintaining paperwork are easily accomplished with this menu.

Short time period. This menu is intended for shorter periods of time, from one day to one week in the primary classroom.

Limitations

Few topics. This menu only covers one or three topics.

Time Considerations

This menu usually is intended for shorter periods of completion time—at most, it should take one week in a primary inclusive classroom. If the menu focuses on one topic in depth, it can be completed in 1–2 days.

TIC-TAC-TOE MENU

"At first, I thought it was a game, but it was really work—but then it was fun like a game."

—First-grade on-level student

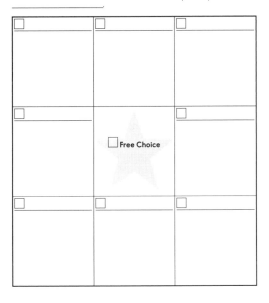

TITLE

Directions: Check the boxes you plan to complete. They should form a tic-tac-toe across or down. All activities must be completed by

☐ Free Choice

Figure 3. Tic-Tac-Toe menu example.

Description

The Tic-Tac-Toe menu (see Figure 3) is a well-known, commonly used target-based menu that contains a total of eight predetermined choices and, if appropriate, one free choice for students. Choices can be created at the same level of Bloom's revised taxonomy or be arranged in a way to allow for three different levels or content areas. If all choices have been created at the same level of Bloom's revised taxonomy, each choice carries the same weight for grading and has similar expectations for completion time and effort.

Benefits

Flexibility. This menu can cover either one topic in depth or three different objectives. When this menu covers just one objective, all at the same level of Bloom's Revised taxonomy, students have the option of completing three products in a tic-tac-toe pattern or simply picking three from the menu.

When it covers three objectives or multiple levels of Bloom's revised taxonomy, students will need to complete a tic-tac-toe pattern (one in each column or row) to be sure they have completed one activity from each objective.

Challenge level. When students make choices on this menu to complete a row or column, based on its design, they will usually face one choice that is out of their comfort zone, be it for its level of Bloom's revised taxonomy, its product learning style, or its content. They will complete this "uncomfortable" choice because they want to do the other two options in that row or column.

Friendly design. Students quickly understand how to use this menu. It is nonthreatening because it does not contain points, therefore it seems to encourage students to stretch out of their comfort zones.

Weighting. All products are equally weighted, so recording grades and maintaining paperwork are easily accomplished with this menu.

Short time period. This menu is intended for shorter periods of time, between 1–3 weeks, although in a self-contained primary classroom, they can be completed within one week.

Limitations

Ease of modification. This menu does not lend itself to reducing the number of options that inclusive children often need when first approaching choice. It may not be as appropriate for a starter menu with these children.

Few topics. This menu only covers one or three topics.

Student compromise. Although this menu does allow for choice, a student will sometimes have to compromise and complete an activity he or she would not have chosen because it completes the required tic-tac-toe. (This is not always bad, though!)

Time Considerations

This menu usually is intended for shorter periods of completion time—at most, it should take 2–3 weeks in a primary inclusive classroom, with one product submitted each week. If the menu focuses on one topic in depth, it can be completed in one week.

PICK 3 MENU

"I started with the Pick 3 menu, although I just had my students pick any two—I wasn't too sure about jumping into three for their first menu. Most had no problem and wanted to do even more."

—First-grade teacher

TITLE

Directions: Circle three activities you would like to do. Color in the square after you are finished.

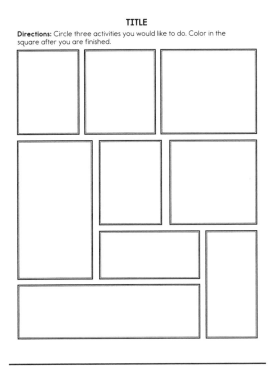

Figure 4. Pick 3 menu example.

Description

The Pick 3 menu (see Figure 4) is a target-based menu that has a total of at least eight predetermined choices. These choices are placed randomly on the page, allowing students to select the target number as determined by the teachers. Choices are provided from different learning styles, as well as different levels of Bloom's revised taxonomy.

Benefits

Ease of modification. If the target number is three, the menu can be divided into three sections and the child selects one from each area. The target number can also easily be modified based on the ability of the child.

Weighting. All products are equally weighted, so recording grades and maintaining paperwork are easily accomplished with this menu.

Challenge level. When this menu is developed with multiple higher level activities, students will complete at least one activity at a higher level of Bloom's revised taxonomy in order to reach their target goal.

Intimidation level. The format of this menu is very student friendly, as it resembles other enjoyable activities often found at the primary grade levels.

Limitations

Few topics. This menu is best used for one topic in depth, although it can be used for up to three different topics, depending on its organization.

Cannot guarantee objectives. If the menu is used for more than one topic, it is possible for a student not to complete an activity for each objective, depending on the choices he or she makes.

Preparation. Teachers need to have all of the materials ready at the beginning of the unit for students to be able to choose any of the activities on the menu, which requires advanced planning.

Time Considerations

This menu usually is intended for shorter periods of completion time—at most, one week in a primary inclusive classroom.

TARGET-BASED LIST MENU

"I didn't think I would like it. It looked really hard but it was OK. I even got to use the computer to make something."

—Second-grade on-level student

Description

The Target-Based List menu (see Figure 5) has a total of at least 10 predetermined choices and at least one free choice for students. Choices are listed in such a way that all of the options are similar levels of Bloom's revised taxonomy, and the student is expected to complete a minimum number of activities.

Benefits

Ease of modification. Although the modification of this menu is not obvious, using a dark marker, teachers can divide the menu into smaller chunks. If the target number is three, the menu can be divided into three sections, and the child will select one from each area. The target number can also easily be modified based on the ability of the child.

Weighting. All products are equally weighted, so recording grades and maintaining paperwork are easily accomplished with this menu.

TITLE

Directions:
1. You may complete as many of the activities listed as you can within the time period.
2. You may choose any combination of activities. Your goal is to complete _____ activities.
3. You may be as creative as you like within the guidelines listed below.
4. You must share your plan with your teacher by _____.

Plan to Do	Activity to Complete	Completed
	Total number of activities you are planning to complete:	Total number of activities completed:

I am planning to complete ____ activities.

Teacher's initials _____ Student's signature _____

Figure 5. Target-Based List menu example.

Challenge level. When this menu is developed with multiple higher level activities, students will complete at least one activity at a higher level of Bloom's revised taxonomy in order to reach their target goal.

Limitations

Few topics. This menu is best used for one topic in depth, although it can be used for up to three different topics, depending on its organization.

Cannot guarantee objectives. If this menu is used for more than one topic, it is possible for a student not to have to complete an activity for each objective, depending on the choices he or she makes.

Preparation. Teachers need to have all of the materials ready at the beginning of the unit for students to be able to choose any of the activities on the list, which requires advanced planning.

Time Considerations

This menu usually is intended for shorter periods of completion time—at most, 2 weeks in a primary inclusive classroom.

GIVE ME 5 MENU

"I really liked the Give Me 5. I used it in February as my first 'real' menu. The students understood the goal of 5 and the choices were limited enough that it didn't overwhelm them—even my lowest [students] were successful."

—Kindergarten teacher

Description

A Give Me 5 point-based menu (see Figure 6) has activities worth two, three, or five points. It is a shorter variation on the 2-5-8 menu, with a total of at least six predetermined choices: at least two choices with a point value of two, at least two choices with a point value of three, and at least two choices with a point value of five. Choices are assigned these points based on the levels of Bloom's revised taxonomy. Choices with a point value of two represent the *remember* and *understand* levels; choices with a point value of three represent the *apply* and *analyze* levels; and choices with a point value of five represent the *evaluate* and *create* levels. Each level of choice carries different weights and has different expectations for completion time and effort. Students are expected to

Figure 6. Give Me 5 menu example.

earn five points for a 100%, and they choose what combination they would like to use to attain that point goal. As with the 2-5-8 menu (see below), early primary teachers usually develop a way for students to understand their progress toward their point goals. Some will have students color the graphics along the bottom of the menu as they complete different point values, and some will give pennies, tokens, or tickets as each product is completed so students can see the concrete results of their efforts.

Benefits

Ease of modification. Being point-based, this menu allows the teacher and students to contract for different point values based on modifications, time constraints, and abilities. For example, rather than five points, a student with special needs could be given a goal of three as the target point value for 100%.

Responsibility. With this menu, students have complete control over their grades and/or how they reach their goals or target numbers. Although grades are not always a focus for students at the primary levels, it is a benefit for them to understand the basis of working toward a goal, be it a grade or a target number.

Appropriate challenge level. This menu's design is set up in such a way that students must complete at least one activity at a higher level of Bloom's revised taxonomy in order to reach their point goal; however, there is enough support to allow students with special needs to work their way up to the higher level with appropriate products.

Limitations

One topic. Although this menu can be used for more than one topic, it works best with in-depth study of one topic.

No free choice. By nature, it also does not allow students to propose their own free-choice activity, because point values need to be assigned based on Bloom's revised taxonomy.

Time Considerations

This menu usually is intended for shorter periods of completion time— at most, one week in a primary inclusive classroom; most self-contained teachers can complete this menu in 1–2 days.

2-5-8 MENU

"[The 2-5-8 menu] was fun. I got my 10 tickets and everything!"

—Kindergarten student

Description

A 2-5-8 menu (see Figure 7) is a point-based menu that is a longer version of the Give Me 5 menu; it has activities worth two, five, or eight points. It has a total of at least eight predetermined choices: at least two choices with a point value of two, at least four choices with a point value of five, and at least two choices with a point value of eight. Choices are assigned these point values based on the levels of Bloom's revised taxonomy. Choices with a point value of two represent the *remember* and *understand* levels; choices with a point value of five represent the *apply* and *analyze* levels; and choices with a point value of eight represent the *evaluate* and *create* levels. Each level of choice carries different weights and has different expectations for completion time and effort.

Students are expected to earn 10 points for a 100%, and they choose what combination they would like to use to attain that point goal. Early primary teachers usually develop a way for students to understand their progress toward their point goal. As with the Give Me 5 menu, some teachers will have students color the graphics along the bottom of the menu as they complete different point values, and some will give pennies, tokens, or tickets as each product is completed so students can see the concrete results of their efforts.

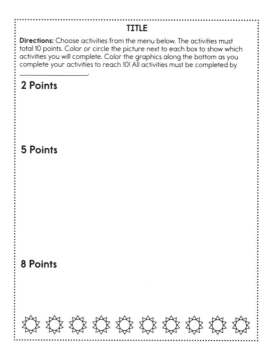

Figure 7. 2-5-8 menu example.

Benefits

Ease of modification. Being point-based, this menu allows the teacher and students to contract for different point values based on modifications, time constraints, and abilities. For example, rather than 10 points, a student with special needs could be given a goal of eight as the target point value for 100%.

Responsibility. With this menu, students have complete control over their grade and/or how they reach their goal or target number. Although grades are not always a focus for students at the primary levels, it is a benefit for them to understand the basis of working toward a goal, be it a grade or a target number.

Challenge level. This menu's design is set up in such a way that students must complete at least one activity at a higher level of Bloom's revised taxonomy in order to reach their point goal.

Limitations

One topic. Although this menu can be used for more than one topic, it works best with in-depth study of one topic.

No free choice. By nature, the menu does not automatically allow students to propose their own free choices, although it can be incorporated as a five- or eight-point option.

Limited challenge level. Students will complete only one activity at a higher level of thinking or, if contracted for other point values, could avoid the higher thinking options altogether.

Time Considerations

This menu usually is intended for shorter periods of completion time—at most, one week in a primary inclusive classroom.

FREE CHOICE IN THE INCLUSIVE PRIMARY CLASSROOM

"I decided to not include free choice on my menus until right before the end of the year. [The students] just weren't ready. I had a few do some neat projects though when I did."

—First-grade teacher

Many of the menus included in this book allow students to submit a free-choice product. This is a product of their choosing that addresses the content being studied and shows what the student has learned about the topic. Although this option is available, students may not fully understand its benefits or immediately respond to the opportunity even after it has been explained. In the past, certain students may have been offered choices and enjoyed the idea of taking charge of their own learning, however, students with special needs may not have had much exposure to this concept. Their educational experiences tend to be objective based and teacher-driven. This is not to say that they would not respond well to the idea of free choice; in fact, they can embrace it enthusiastically. Students with special needs need to feel confident in their knowledge of the content and information before they are ready to step out on their own, propose their own ideas, and create their own products.

Figure 8 shows two sample proposal forms that have been used successfully with primary students when the students are allowed to submit a free choice for their teacher's consideration. If the teacher has decided that his or her students have had enough exposure to different products and are ready to work independently, a copy of these forms can be given to each student when a menu that includes a free choice option is first intro-

Name: _____ Teacher's Approval: _____

FREE-CHOICE PROPOSAL FORM

Proposal Outline

1. What will you learn about? _____

_____

_____

2. What will it look like? _____

_____

_____

3. What will you need from the teacher to make it? _____

_____

Name: _____ Teacher's Approval: _____

FREE-CHOICE PROPOSAL FORM
FOR POINT-BASED MENU

I want to create something for _____ points.   Points Approval: _____

Proposal Outline

1. What will you learn about? _____

_____

2. What will it look like? _____

_____

_____

3. What will you need from the teacher to make it? _____

_____

Figure 8. Sample proposal forms for free choice.

duced. The form used is based on the type of menu being presented. For example, if you are using the Tic-Tac-Toe or Meal menu, there is no need to submit a point proposal.

A discussion should be held with the students so they understand the expectations of a free choice. There are always a few students who do not want to complete a task on the menu or have their own idea of what they would like to do; they are welcome to create their own free choice product and submit it for approval. The more free choice is used and encouraged, the more students will begin to request it. How the students show their knowledge will begin to shift from teacher-focused to student-designed activities. If students do not want to make a proposal using the proposal form after the teacher has discussed the entire menu and its activities, they can place the unused form in a designated place in the classroom. Others may want to use the form, and it is often surprising who wants to submit a proposal form after hearing about the opportunity.

Proposal forms must be submitted before students begin working on their free-choice products. The teacher then knows what the students are working on, and the students know the expectations the teacher has for their products. Once approved, the forms can be stapled to the students' menu sheets. The students can refer to their own form as they develop their free-choice product, and when the grading takes place, the teacher can refer to the agreement for the graded features of the product.

As a note, although all of the above considerations rely on the students to complete their own proposal form, this should not deter students whose writing skills are not at the same level as their verbal skills. Although it would be wonderful if all of the children could complete and submit their own proposal forms, that is not always the case. In fact, those students who have strong verbal and artistic skills may want to create a product that showcases their ability but the proposal form itself hinders them. After discussing the option of free choice, it is always recommended that the teacher offer to help students fill out their free-choice form if there is something else that they would really like to create. When children who are struggling are temporarily freed from a written task, it is amazing what they can create to show their learning.

Each part of the proposal form is important and needs to be discussed with students.

- *Name/Teacher's Approval.* The student or teacher will fill in the student's name. The student must submit this form to the teacher for approval. The teacher will carefully review all of the information, discuss any suggestions or alterations with the student, if needed, and then sign the top.

- *Points Requested.* Found only on the point-based menu proposal form, this is where negotiation may need to take place. Students usually will submit their first request for a very high number (even the 100% goal). They tend to equate the amount of time something will take with the number of points it should earn. But please note that the points are always based on the levels of Bloom's revised taxonomy and its appropriate alignment with the student's age and ability level. For example, students may be asked to apply what they know to a new situation, perhaps by making a set of concentration cards about animals they have not studied. This would be a higher level activity for a kindergarten student, but a middle-level activity for a second grader because Bloom's revised taxonomy is developmental in nature.

- *Points Approved.* Found only on the point-based menu proposal form, this is the final decision recorded by the teacher once the point haggling is finished.

- *Proposal Outline.* This is where the student will describe the product he or she intends to complete. Primary students may need some assistance refining and narrowing their ideas. Teachers should ask questions to understand what students plan to complete, as well as to ensure student understanding. This also shows the teacher that the student knows what he or she is planning on completing.

    o *What will you learn about?* Students need to be specific here. It is not acceptable to write *science* or *reading*. This is where they look at the objectives of the product and choose which objective their product demonstrates.

    o *What will it look like?* It is important for this section to be as detailed as possible. If a student cannot express what the product will look like, he or she probably has not given the free-choice plan enough thought.

    o *What will you need from the teacher to make it?* This is an important consideration. Sometimes students do not have the means to purchase items for their product. This can be negotiated, but if teachers ask students to think about what they may need, they will often develop even grander ideas for their free choice product.

CHAPTER 2

How to Use Menus in the Inclusive Primary Classroom

There are different ways to use instructional product-based menus in the inclusive classroom. In order to decide how to implement each menu, the following questions should be considered: How much prior knowledge of the topic being taught do the students have before the unit or lesson begins, how confident are your students in making choices and working independently, and how much intellectually and/or developmentally appropriate information is readily available for students to obtain on their own? After considering these questions, there are a variety of ways to use menus in the classroom.

RECALLING OR BUILDING BACKGROUND KNOWLEDGE

There are many ways to use menus in the classroom. One way that is often overlooked is using menus to review or build background knowledge before a unit begins. This is frequently used when first- and second-grade students have had exposure to upcoming content in the past, perhaps during the previous year's instruction or through similar life experiences. Although they may have been exposed to the content previously, students may not remember the details of the content at the level needed to proceed with this year's unit immediately. A shorter menu covering the previous year's objectives can be provided in the day or week prior to the new unit so that students have the opportunity to recall and engage with the information in a meaningful way. They will then be ready to take their knowledge to a deeper level during the unit. For example, a few days before starting a unit on alphabet books, the teacher may select a short menu on the alphabet, knowing that the students have had the content in the past and should be able to successfully work independently on the menu by engaging their prior knowledge. Students work on basic products from the menu as anchor activities throughout the week preceding the alphabet book unit, with all products being submitted prior to the unit's initiation. This way, the students have been in the "letter frame of mind" independently for a week and are ready to investigate the topic further.

ENRICHMENT AND SUPPLEMENTAL ACTIVITIES

Using the menus for enrichment and supplemental activities is the most common way of using menus. In this case, the students usually do not have a lot of background knowledge, and information about the topic may not be readily available to all students. The teacher will introduce the menu and the activities at the beginning of a unit. The teacher then will progress through the content at the normal rate using his or her curricular materials, periodically allowing class and perhaps center time throughout the unit for students to work on their menu choices to supplement the lessons being taught. This method is very effective, as it incorporates an immediate use for the content the teacher is covering. For example, at the beginning of a unit on animals, the teacher may introduce the menu with the explanation that students may not yet have enough knowledge to complete all of their choices. During the unit, however, more content will be provided and the students will be prepared to work on new choices. If students want to work ahead, they can certainly find the information on their own, but that is not required. Although some students often see this as a challenge and will begin to investigate concepts mentioned in the menu before the teacher has discussed them, other students begin to develop questions about the concepts and are ready to ask them when the teacher covers the material. This helps build an immense pool of background knowledge and possible content questions before the topic is even discussed in the classroom. This way, primary students are more likely to be excited about the topic and are ready to discuss and question the new content as it is presented. By introducing a menu at the beginning of a unit and allowing students to complete products as instruction progresses, we encourage the students to naturally investigate the information and come to class prepared.

COMPACTING

Within any primary classroom, there are diverse knowledge and ability levels that can vary based on the content being studied or even the topic within a content. Compacting, or preassessing students and then offering alternatives for any student who shows mastery, is often used to address these diverse abilities. Given the task of compacting curricular units, teachers are often frustrated by locating alternative options to replace certain activities and lessons for those students who have "tested out." A common solution is setting up a preassessment with the stipulation that only if a student tests out of a unit completely will an alternate assignment be available, thereby decreasing the number of alternative options a teacher would need to find or create. This solution, although practical, may guarantee that students with special needs never have the opportunity to compact their learning, even for a unit for which they may have a lot of knowledge. The best model of compacting allows students, no matter their ability level, who show proficiency in just one piece or aspect of the unit of study to complete an alternate assignment. Menus can be used to serve this purpose. Whether students test out of an entire unit that is their passion area or show proficiency in just one aspect, activities can be selected and offered to replace the standard instruction. If the entire class has access to the menu for enrichment, students whose curricula have been compacted may be contracted to choose between certain options to be completed, thereby replacing the planned curricular activities that they have already mastered.

STANDARD ACTIVITIES

Another option for using menus in the classroom is to replace certain curricular activities the teacher uses to teach the specified content. In this case, the students may have some limited background knowledge about the content, and appropriately leveled information is readily available for them in their classroom resources. The teacher would pick and choose which aspects of the content must be directly taught to the students and which could be appropriately learned and reinforced through product menus. The unit would then be designed using a mixture of formal large-group lessons, small-group lessons, and specific menu times (often through centers) where the students would use the menu to reinforce their prior knowledge. In order for this option to be effective, the teacher must feel very comfortable with the students' prior knowledge level. Although there are a few occasions when menus could be used this way with Kindergarten students, this is more for second-semester first and second graders.

Another variation on this method that is appropriate for Kindergarten students is using the menus to drive center activities. Centers have many different functions in the classroom—most importantly, reinforcing the instruction that has taken place. Rather than having a set rotation for centers, the teacher could use the menu activities as enrichment or supplemental activities during center time for those students who need more than just reinforcement; centers could be set up with any materials students would need to complete their products.

CHAPTER 3

Product Guidelines

"I just don't know what I want to do. Maybe something with markers."

—Kindergarten student

This chapter outlines the different types of products included in the featured menus, as well as the guidelines and expectations for each. It is very important that students know the expectations of a completed product when they choose to work on it. By discussing and demonstrating these expectations *before* students begin, and by having information readily available for students, the teacher can limit frustration on everyone's part.

It is very important to note that when using the product guidelines—or products in general—with primary inclusive students, the students need to have some experience with the product in a whole-class setting before being asked to create their own. This means that the teacher may need to spend some time during the first weeks of school integrating the types of products into lessons that the students will encounter in their menus later on in the year. The guidelines will then simply serve as a visual clue to remind the children about the product outlined in the task.

$1 CONTRACT

I did not spend more than $1.00 on my _____

_____   _____
                    Student Signature   Date

My child, _____, did not spend more than $1.00 on the product he or she created.

_____   _____
                    Parent Signature   Date

Figure 9. $1 contract example.

$1 CONTRACT

Consideration should be given to the cost of creating the products featured on any menu. The resources available to students vary within a classroom, and students should not be graded on the amount of materials they can purchase to make their products look better. These menus are designed to equalize the resources students have available. The materials for most products are available for less than a dollar and can usually be found in a teacher's classroom as part of the classroom supplies. If a product requires materials from the student, there is a $1 contract as part of the product criteria. This is a very important part of the explanation of the product. First of all, limiting the amount of money a child (or his or her parents) can spend creates an equal amount of resources for all students. Second, it actually encourages a more creative product. When students are limited by the amount of materials they can readily purchase, they often have to use materials from home in new and unique ways. Figure 9 shows a sample $1 contract that has been used many times in my classroom for various products.

THE PRODUCTS

Table 1 contains a list of the products used in this book and additional products that can be used as free-choice ideas. These products were chosen for their flexibility in meeting learning styles, for their appropriateness for primary students, and for being products many teachers already encourage in their classrooms. They have been arranged by learning style—visual, kinesthetic, and auditory—and each menu has been designed to include products appropriate for all learning styles. Some of the best products cross over between different categories; however, they have been listed here by how they are presented or implemented in the menus.

Product Frustrations

One of the biggest frustrations that accompany the use of these various products on the menus is the barrage of questions about the products themselves. Students can become so wrapped up in the products and the criteria for creating them that they do not focus on the content being presented. This is especially true when menus are first introduced to the class. Students can spend an exorbitant amount of time asking the teacher about the products mentioned on a menu. When this happens, what should have been a 10–15-minute menu introduction turns into 45–50 minutes of discussion about product expectations. In order to facilitate the introduction of the menu products, teachers should have on hand examples of the products students have already created with guidance from the teacher. This, in addition to the product guideline, is usually enough to trigger their memory about a specific product.

Teachers may consider showing students examples of the product(s) from the previous year. Although this can be helpful, it can also lead to additional frustration on the part of both the teacher and the students. Some students may not feel that they can produce a product as nice, as big, as special, or as (you fill in the blank) as the example, or when shown an example, students might interpret that as meaning that the teacher would like something exactly like the one he or she showed to students. To avoid this situation, I would propose that when using examples, the example students are shown be a "blank" one that demonstrates how to create only the shell of the product. If an example of a windowpane is needed, for instance, students might be shown a blank piece of paper that is divided into six panes. The students can then take the skeleton of the product and

Table 1
PRODUCTS

Visual	Kinesthetic	Auditory
Acrostic	Board Game	Children's Book
Advertisement	Bulletin Board Display	Commercial
Book Cover	Class Game	Demonstration
Brochure/Pamphlet	Collection	News Report
Bulletin Board Display	Commercial	Play/Skit
Cartoon/Comic Strip	Concentration Cards	PowerPoint–
Children's Book	Cube	Presentation
Collage	Demonstration	Presentation of Created
Crossword Puzzle	Diorama	Product
Diary/Journal	Flipbook	Puppet
Drawing	Folded Quiz Book	Song/Rap
Essay/Research Report	Jigsaw Puzzle	Speech
Folded Quiz Book	Mobile	Tell a Story
Greeting Card	Model	You Be the Person
Instruction Card	Mural	Presentation
Letter	Mystery Object	
List	Play/Skit	
Map	Puppet	
Mind Map	Show and Tell	
Newspaper Article		
Paragraph		
Picture Dictionary		
Poster		
PowerPoint–Stand Alone		
Scrapbook		
Story–Written		
Trading Cards		
Venn Diagram		
Windowpane		

make it their own as they create their own version of the windowpane using their information.

Product Guidelines

Most frustrations associated with products can be addressed proactively through the introduction of the product in a whole-class setting and the use of standardized, predetermined product guidelines that are shared with students prior to them creating any products. These product guidelines are designed in a specific yet generic way, such that any time throughout the school year that the students select a product, that product's guidelines will apply. A beneficial side effect of using set guidelines for a product is the security it creates. Students are often reticent to try something new, as doing so requires taking a risk. Traditionally, when students select a product, they ask questions about creating it, hope they remember and understood all of the details, and turn it in. It can be quite a surprise when they receive the product back and realize that it was not complete or was not what was expected. As you can imagine, students may not want to take a risk on something new the next time; they often prefer to do what they know and be successful. Through the use of product guidelines, students can begin to feel secure in their choice before they start working on a new product. If they are not feeling secure, they tend to stay within their comfort zone.

The product guidelines for menu products included in this book, as well as some potential free-choice options, are included in an easy-to-read card format that was selected especially for inclusive students (see Figure 10) with a graphic that depicts the guidelines for each product. (The guidelines for some products, such as presentation of created product, are omitted because teachers often have their own criteria for these products.) These guideline cards are convenient for students to have in front of them when they work on their products. Each card has a graphic that should trigger their recall of the product they have previously created with their teacher as well as illustrate most of the important criteria stated on the product card. These graphics are also found on each menu. They are the focal point of the lower level menus ▲, which have fewer words, and the graphics are next to the task statements that require the corresponding product on the on-level menus ●. This allows students to easily match a product with its criteria if teachers are using the product guidelines.

There really is no one right way to share the product guideline information with your students. It all depends on their abilities and needs. Some second-grade teachers choose to duplicate and distribute all of the product guidelines pages to students at the beginning of the year so each child has his or her own copy while working on products. As another option, a few classroom sets can be created by gluing each product guideline card onto a separate index card, hole punching the corner of each card, and placing all of the cards on a metal ring. These ring sets can be placed in a central location or at centers where students can borrow and return them as they work on their products. This allows for the addition of products as they are introduced. Some teachers prefer to introduce the product guidelines and their specific graphics as students experience products through whole-class activities. In this case, the product guidelines may be enlarged, laminated, and posted on a bulletin board for easy access and reference during classroom work. Some teachers prefer to give only a few product guidelines at a time, while others may feel it is appropriate to provide more cards when students start feeling comfortable enough to develop their own free choice products. The cards for the products mentioned in a specific menu can also be reduced in size and copied onto the back of that menu so they are available when students want to refer to them. Students enjoy looking at all of the different product options, and they may get new ideas as they peruse the guidelines. No matter which method teachers choose to share the information with the students, they will save themselves a lot of time and frustration by having the product guidelines available for student reference (e.g., "Look at your product guidelines—I think that will answer your question").

ACROSTIC

- White piece of paper
- Written neatly
- Main word on the left-hand side
- 1 phrase for each letter
- Phrases must be about the main word

ADVERTISEMENT

- White piece of paper
- Draw and color the picture of item or service
- Include price, if needed

BOARD GAME

- At least 4 game pieces
- At least 20 colored squares
- At least 10 question cards
- Title of the game on the game board
- Explain rules of the game
- At least the size of a file folder

BOOK COVER

- Front cover—include title, author, and picture
- Cover inside flap—write a paragraph or sentences about the book
- Back inside flap—provide information about the author with at least 3 facts
- Back cover—tell whether you liked the book and why
- Spine—include title and author

Figure 10. Product guidelines.

BROCHURE/PAMPHLET

- White piece of paper
- Fold the paper
- Title and picture on the front page
- At least 5 facts inside

BULLETIN BOARD DISPLAY

- Has to fit on a bulletin board or wall
- At least 5 facts
- Has a title
- Needs to be creative

CARTOON/COMIC STRIP

- White piece of paper
- At least 6 squares or cells
- Have characters talk to each other
- Use color

CHILDREN'S BOOK

- Cover with the title and your name
- At least 10 pages
- Picture on each page
- Written neatly

Figure 10. Continued.

CLASS GAME

- Needs easy rules
- Include questions for your classmates
- Can be like a game you know how to play

COLLAGE

- White piece of paper
- Cut pictures neatly
- Use magazines or newspapers
- Glue pictures neatly on the paper
- Label pictures

COLLECTION

- Has the number of items needed
- Fit items inside area
- Bring in a box or bag
- No living things

COMMERCIAL

- 1–2 minutes in length
- Presented to classmates or recorded ahead of time
- Use props or costumes
- Can have more than 1 person in it

Figure 10. Continued.

CONCENTRATION CARDS

- At least 20 cards (10 matching sets)
- Has pictures, words, or both
- Write on only 1 side of each card
- Include an answer key that shows the matches
- In a bag or envelope

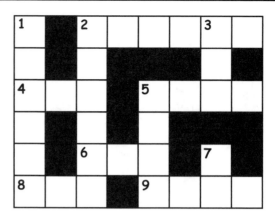

CROSSWORD PUZZLE

- At least 15 words
- Provide clues for each word
- Include puzzle and answer key
- Can be made on the computer

CUBE

- Use all 6 sides of the cube to provide information
- Written neatly or made on the computer
- Print your name neatly on the bottom of 1 of the sides
- Should be turned in flat (unfolded) for grading

DEMONSTRATION

- At least 1 minute
- Show all important information
- Include 2 questions for classmates
- Be able to answer questions from classmates

Figure 10. Continued.

DIARY/JOURNAL

- Written neatly or made on the computer
- Write at least 1 page for each day
- Has the date on each page
- Write as if you are the character

DIORAMA

- Use a box
- Glue pictures and information on the inside walls of box
- Write your name on the back
- Write information about the diorama on a card
- Fill out a $1 contract

DRAWING

- White piece of paper
- Use colors
- Drawn neatly
- Has a title
- Write your name on the back

ESSAY/RESEARCH REPORT

- Written neatly or made on the computer
- Includes enough information about the topic
- Write the information in your own words (no copying from books or the Internet!)

Figure 10. Continued.

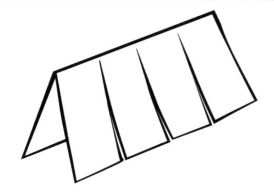

FLIPBOOK

- White piece of paper folded in half
- Cut flaps into the top
- Use color for the drawings
- Write your name on the back

FOLDED QUIZ BOOK

- Folded white paper
- At least 8 questions
- Write the questions on the outside flaps
- Write the answers inside each flap
- Write your name on the back

GREETING CARD

- Front—include colored pictures (words are optional)
- Front inside—include a personal note
- Back inside—include a greeting, saying, or poem
- Back outside—include your name and price of card

INSTRUCTION CARD

- Use large blank or lined index card
- Written neatly or made on the computer
- Use color for drawings
- Provide clear instructions

Figure 10. Continued.

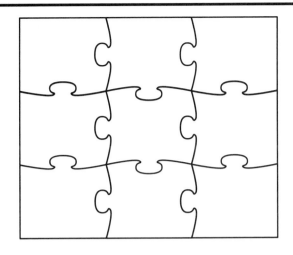

JIGSAW PUZZLE

- Use cardstock
- At least 9 pieces
- Use color
- May have words
- Makes a picture when finished

LETTER

- Written neatly or made on the computer
- Follow letter format
- Include all needed information

LIST

- Written neatly or made on the computer
- Include the number of items required
- Very complete
- Include words or phrases for each letter of alphabet except X for alphabet lists

MAP

- White piece of paper
- Information is correct and accurate
- At least 8 locations
- Include a compass rose, legend, scale, and key

Figure 10. Continued.

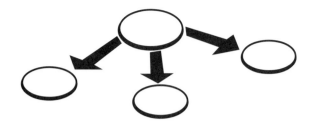

MIND MAP

- White piece of unlined paper
- 1 word in the middle
- No more than 4 words coming from any 1 word
- Written neatly or made on the computer

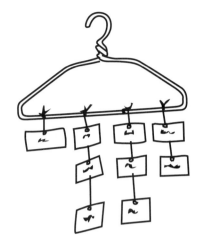

MOBILE

- At least 10 pieces of information
- Include color and pictures
- Include at least 3 layers of hanging information
- Hangs straight

MODEL

- At least 8" × 8" × 12"
- Label the parts of the model
- Include a title card
- Use recycled materials
- Write your name on the model

MURAL

- Size of a poster board or bigger
- At least 5 pieces of information
- Color the pictures on the mural
- May include words; must include a title
- Write your name on the back

Figure 10. Continued.

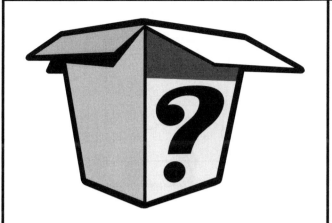

MYSTERY OBJECT

- Put your object in a box
- At least 4 clues so others can guess
- No living things

NEWS REPORT

- Tell who, what, where, when, why, and how the event happened
- Can be presented to classmates or recorded ahead of time

NEWSPAPER ARTICLE

- Should describe what happened
- Design it to look like a newspaper article
- Include a picture to go with article
- Include all relevant information
- Written neatly or made on the computer

The sky is blue today. I see a boat on the lake and a man fishing. There is a bird singing in the tree outside my window. I will soon eat breakfast and go for a bike ride with my friend Julie. It is a good day.

PARAGRAPH

- Written neatly or made on the computer
- Must have topic sentence, at least 3 supporting sentences or details, and a concluding sentence
- Must use vocabulary and punctuation

Figure 10. Continued.

PICTURE DICTIONARY

- Written neatly or made on the computer
- Have a clear picture for each word
- Draw pictures
- Use your own words for definitions

PLAY/SKIT

- 3–5 minutes in length
- Turn in written script before play is presented
- Present to classmates or record ahead of time
- Use props or costumes
- Can have more than 1 person in it

POSTER

- Use poster board
- At least 5 pieces of important information
- Must have a title
- Use both words and pictures
- Write your name on the back
- Include a bibliography as needed

POWERPOINT– PRESENTATION

- At least 8 slides, plus a title slide with your name
- Use color in slides
- No more than 1 picture per page
- Can use animation, but limit it
- Should be timed to flow with the oral presentation

Figure 10. Continued.

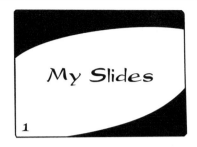

POWERPOINT— STAND ALONE

- At least 8 slides, plus a title slide with your name
- Use color in slides
- No more than 10 words on each page
- No more than 1 picture per page
- Can use animation, but limit how much

PUPPET

- Should be handmade and have a moveable mouth
- List supplies used to make the puppet
- Use recycled materials
- Sign a $1 contract
- If used in a play, all play criteria must be met as well

SCRAPBOOK

- Include a meaningful title and your name on the cover
- At least 4 pages in length
- At least 1 picture on each page
- Captions for all pictures

SHOW AND TELL

- Bring 1 thing to school
- Tell 3 things about it
- Answer at least 1 question

Figure 10. Continued.

SONG/RAP

- At least 1 minute in length
- Should be able to understand all words in the song/rap
- Can be a familiar tune
- Can be presented to classmates or recorded ahead of time
- Turn in written words

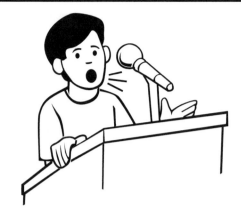

SPEECH

- At least 1 minute in length
- Speak clearly and loudly
- Try not to read directly from your paper
- Turn in the written speech before you speak

STORY—WRITTEN

- Include all of the elements of a well-written story
- Should be long enough for the story to make sense
- Written neatly or made on the computer

TELL A STORY

- Include all of the elements of a well-written story
- Should be long enough for the story to make sense
- Told to teacher or recorded on a computer

Figure 10. Continued.

TRADING CARDS

- At least 8 cards
- At least 3" × 5"
- Colored picture on each card
- At least 3 facts on each card
- Can have information on both sides
- Turn in cards in a carrying bag

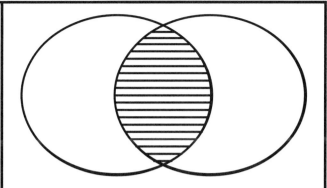

VENN DIAGRAM

- A piece of paper turned lengthwise
- Include a title at the top
- Include a title for each circle
- At least 6 items in each part

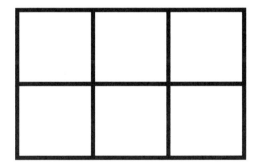

WINDOWPANE

- White piece of paper
- At least 6 squares
- Include a picture and words in each square
- Written neatly or made on the computer
- Be creative
- Write your name on the back

YOU BE THE PERSON PRESENTATION

- Pretend to be the person
- 1–3 minutes in length
- At least 5 facts about his or her life
- Present to classmates
- Be able to answer questions about your character
- Use props or a costume

Figure 10. Continued.

USING STORY MAPS

One of the most commonly used products in language arts is the story map. The story map is a quick and effective way for a student to dissect a story and show that he or she can analyze the important parts. Story maps are an option for many of the menus provided in this book. They also are included when students are asked to write a story; this provides students a place to start in the organization of their own writing. Of course, story map expectations and, subsequently, the format that would be appropriate are dependent on the abilities and analytical level of each child. Two examples are offered to accommodate these different ability levels (see Figures 11 ▲ and 12 ●); however, teachers who have a favorite format that students are accustomed to should feel free to use their own.

BEGINNING, MIDDLE, AND END STORY MAP   ▲

Title_____

_____

Author _____

Illustrator _____

Beginning of the Story

_____

_____

_____

_____

Middle of the Story

_____

_____

_____

_____

_____

_____

End of the Story

_____

_____

_____

_____

Figure 11. Beginning, middle, and end story map.

STORY MAP

●

Title_____

_____

Author _____

Illustrator _____

Setting of Story

_____

_____

_____

_____

Characters in the Story
Write the characters' names and describe each one.

_____

_____

_____

_____

Events in the Story
Write the events in the story and describe each one.

_____

_____

_____

_____

_____

Figure 12. Story map.

CHAPTER 4

Rubrics and Grading

"I think rubrics are important, although we do not really focus on number grades first semester. I think they do share my expectations and it is not a bad thing for the students to understand the concept of expectations."

—First-grade teacher, when asked about the importance of rubrics

The most common reason teachers feel uncomfortable with menus is the need for equal grading. Teachers often feel that it is easier to grade the same type of product made by all of the students than to grade a large number of different products, none of which looks like any other. The great equalizer for hundreds of different products is a generic rubric that can cover all of the important qualities of an excellent product.

ALL-PURPOSE RUBRIC

When it comes to primary students and rubrics, it is often difficult to find a format that is effective in enhancing students' products. The purpose of a rubric is to demonstrate for the students the criteria and expectations of the teacher, as well as to allow the teacher to quickly evaluate a product using these same criteria. When designing a rubric for primary students, it is important to look at what would be meaningful to them. It should also be noted that many kindergarten and first-grade programs do not give formal grades for student work. This should be taken into account when using a rubric.

Figure 14 is an example of a rubric that has been classroom tested in the primary grades with students of various ability levels to encourage quality products. When number grades are assigned, this rubric can be used with any point value activity presented in a point-based menu. When a menu is presented to students, this rubric can be reproduced on the back of the menu with its guidelines or shared with the students along with examples. The first time students see this rubric, it can be explained in detail using the graphics as a guide. This rubric was designed to be specific enough to allow students to understand the criteria the teacher is seeking, but general enough that they can still be as creative as they like in the creation of their products.

ALL-PURPOSE PRODUCT RUBRIC

	Excellent	Good	Poor
Completeness Is everything included in the product?	All information needed is included.	Some important information is missing.	Most important information is missing.
Creativity Is the product original?	Information is creative. Graphics are original.	Information is creative. Graphics are not original or were found on the computer.	There is no evidence of new thoughts or perspectives in the product.
Correctness Is all of the information included correct?	All information in the product is correct and accurate.		Any portion of the information presented is incorrect.
Appropriate Communication Is the information well communicated?	All information is neat, easy to read, and easy to understand if presented.	Most of the product is neat, easy to read, and loud enough if presented.	The product is not neat or it is not easy to read.
Effort and Time Did student put significant effort into the product?	Effort is obvious.		The product does not show significant effort.

Figure 13. All-purpose rubric.

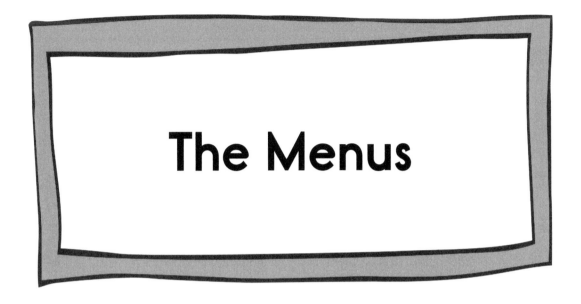

The Menus

HOW TO USE THE MENU PAGES

Each topic in this section has:
- an introduction page for the teacher;
- a lower level content menu, indicated by a triangle ▲ in the upper right-hand corner;
- an on-level content menu, indicated by a circle ● in the upper right-hand corner
- any specific guidelines for the menu, and
- activities mentioned in the menu.

The lower level menus ▲, which are appropriate for lower level readers, include large graphics of the products with fewer words (typically short phrases) to keep the students' focus on the graphics. If a teacher is unsure about a shortened task, a quick glance at the on-level menu ● for that same topic should clarify any questions, as these menus use both graphics and complete sentences to express each task.

INTRODUCTION PAGES

The introduction pages for each topic are meant to provide an overview of each set of menus. They are divided into the following areas:

- *Title and Menu Type*: The top of each introductory page will tell you the main topic covered by the menus as well as the menu type(s) used. Each topic included has two menus, one for lower level students ▲ and one for on-level students ●. In order to modify for students with special needs, the lower level menu focuses more on graphics and may have a different format to control the amount of choice a student faces at one time.

- *Objectives Covered Through These Menus and Activities*. This area will list all of the objectives that the menus address. Menus are arranged in such a way that if students complete the guidelines set forth in the instructions, all of these objectives will be covered. Some objectives may be designated with a ▲ or a ●, which indicates that a particular objective is only addressed on its corresponding menu.

- *Materials Needed by Students for Completion*. For each menu, it is expected that the teacher will provide, or students will have access to, the following materials:
  o lined paper;
  o glue;
  o crayons, colored pencils, or markers; and
  o blank 8.5" × 11" white paper.

  The introduction page also includes a list of additional materials that may be needed by students. Because students have the choice of which menu items they would like to complete, it is possible that the teacher will not need all of the additional materials for every student.

- *Special Notes on the Modifications of These Menus*. Some menu formats have special management issues or considerations when it comes to modifying for different ability levels. This section will review additional options available for modifying a menu.

- *Special Notes on the Use of These Menus*. This section will share any tips to consider for a specific menu format, activity, or product.

- *Time Frame.* Each menu has its own ideal time frame based on its structure, but all menus work best given at least one day or up to a week time frame. Menus that assess more objectives are better suited to time frames of up to 2 weeks. This section will give you an overview about the best time frame for completing the menus, as well as options for shorter time periods. If teachers do not have time to devote to an entire menu, they can certainly choose the one-day option for any topic students are currently studying.
- *Suggested Forms.* This section lists the rubrics that should be available for students as the menus are introduced. If a menu has a free-choice option, the appropriate proposal form will also be listed here.

CHAPTER 5

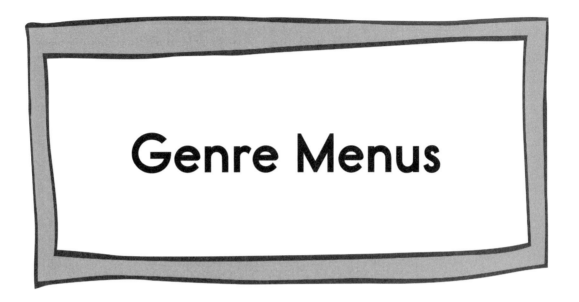

Genre Menus

MY BOOK

MEAL MENU

Reading and Communication Objectives Covered Through This Menu and These Activities

- Students will make predictions based on what is read.
- Students will make inferences from reading.
- Students will show comprehension by retelling or acting out events in a story.
- Students will use both verbal and nonverbal communication.
- Students will present dramatic interpretations of experiences, stories, poems, and plays.
- Students will clarify and support spoken messages using props.
- Students will understand story structure through story maps.
- Students will draw illustrations based on text.
- Students will compare and contrast one literary work with another.
- Students will analyze characters, their relationships, and their importance in the story.
- Students will recognize and analyze story plot and problem resolution.

Writing Objectives Covered Through This Menu and These Activities

- Students will write to record their ideas and reflections.
- Students will generate ideas before writing.
- Students will record their knowledge in a variety of ways.
- Students will write to express their feelings or to reflect.
- Students will write to inform, explain, describe, or narrate.

Materials Needed by Students for Completion

- Poster board or large white paper
- Coat hangers (for mobiles)
- String (for mobiles)
- Blank index cards (for mobiles and trading cards ▲)
- DVD or VHS recorder (for commercials) ●
- Shoeboxes (for dioramas)
- Magazines (for collages)
- Socks (for puppets)

- Paper bags (for puppets)
- Recycled materials (for puppets and dioramas)
- Scrapbooking materials ●
- Materials for board games

Special Notes on the Modifications of These Menus

- The Meal menu format has a design feature that makes it easy to reduce the number of choices students face at one time. Students can be given the left side (breakfast and lunch, or lower levels of thinking) as their first options. After these two meal products have been completed, students can then receive the right side (dinner and dessert, or higher levels of thinking and enrichment options). After becoming accustomed to the amount of choice, students can then get the entire meal menu at once.

Special Notes on the Use of These Menus

- The lower level menu ▲ is specifically designed for students who are lower level readers or for those with a more limited vocabulary. It is meant to simply remind students of product options that have already been explained.
- The on-level menu ● gives students the opportunity to create a commercial. Although students enjoy producing their own videos, there are often difficulties obtaining the equipment and scheduling the use of a video recorder. This activity can be modified by allowing students to act out the commercial (like a play) or, if students have the technology, allowing them to produce a webcam version of their commercial.
- These menus ask students to use recycled materials to create their puppets and dioramas. This does not mean only plastic and paper; instead, students should focus on using materials in new ways. It works well if a box is started for "recycled" contributions at the beginning of the school year. That way, students always have access to these types of materials.

Time Frame

- 1 week—Students are given a menu as the unit is started. As the unit progresses throughout the week, students should refer back to the menu options associated with that content. The teacher will go over all of the options for that content and have students color or circle the graphic for each option that represents the activity they are most interested in completing. As teaching continues, the activities chosen and completed should create a full day's meal, with a breakfast, a lunch, a dinner, and an optional dessert. The teacher may choose to dedicate a learning center to working on menu products or simply allow students time to work after other work is finished. When students complete the menu with this expectation, they have completed one activity from each content area, learning style, or level of Bloom's revised taxonomy, depending on the design of the menu.

- 1–2 days—The teacher chooses an activity or product from an objective to use with the entire class during that lesson time.

Suggested Forms

- All-purpose rubric
- Appropriate story map

MY BOOK

Directions: Choose one activity for breakfast and lunch.

Breakfast

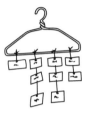

Information about my book

A new cover for my book

You should read my book!

Lunch

My favorite character

The main character of my book

My characters

Directions: Choose one activity for dinner. After you are done with your dinner, you may do a dessert.

Dinner

 The most important scene

 My book

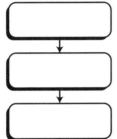 Events from my story

Dessert

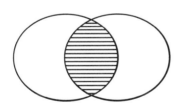 2 books by my author

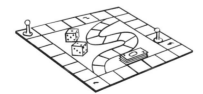 The events in my book

MY BOOK

Directions: Choose one activity for breakfast and lunch.

Breakfast

 Make a **mobile** to share information about your book.

 Create a new **book cover** for your book.

 Write a **commercial** to convince your classmates to read your book.

Lunch

 Think about your favorite character in your book. Design a **collage** about that person.

 Using recycled materials, create a **puppet** of your favorite character.

 Make a **scrapbook** for the adventures of one of your characters.

Directions: Choose one activity for dinner. After you are done with your dinner, you may do a dessert.

Dinner

Using recycled materials, create a **diorama** for the most important scene in your book.

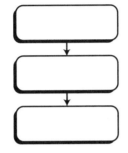

Complete a **story map** for your book.

In a **play**, act out the best scene in your book.

Dessert

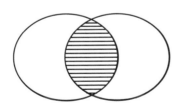

Make a **Venn diagram** to compare and contrast two books by the same author.

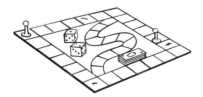

Create a **board game** to go with the events in your book.

CALDECOTT WINNERS

THREE-SHAPE MENU

Reading and Communication Objectives Covered Through This Menu and These Activities

- Students will describe how illustrations contribute to text.
- Students will present dramatic interpretations of experiences, stories, poems, and plays.
- Students will understand story structure through story maps.
- Students will draw illustrations based on text.
- Students will compare and contrast one literary work with another.

Writing Objectives Covered Through This Menu and These Activities

- Students will generate ideas before writing.
- Students will write to inform, explain, describe, or narrate.

Materials Needed by Students for Completion

- Poster board or large white paper
- Caldecott Medal Cube template
- Blank index cards (for trading cards) ▲
- Scrapbooking materials ●
- Socks (for puppets)
- Paper bags (for puppets)
- Recycled materials (for puppets)
- DVD or VHS recorder (for commercials) ●

Special Notes on the Modifications of These Menus

- These two Three-Shape menus have slightly different formats. The lower level menu ▲ has a dotted line with separate instructions for each section. This visually separates the page beyond just the different shapes. This also makes it easy for the teacher to cut the menu as needed based on the comfort level of the students when it comes to choice. If it is the first time choice is being introduced, the children may receive only the strip of square options. Then when they have finished, they can receive the circles and then the diamonds. After students are more accustomed to options, the menu might be cut just once after the circles, so students can select a square and a circle and submit them to the teacher. Then they can choose from the diamond strip they receive. The ultimate goal would be to work up to allowing students to have all nine options at once and not be overwhelmed. The on-level menu ● has one dotted line separating the diamonds from the rest of the menu, making the enrichment options easy to include or cut and distribute later at the teacher's discretion.

Special Notes on the Use of These Menus

- The lower level menu ▲ is specifically designed for students who are lower level readers or for those with a more limited vocabulary. It is meant to simply remind students of product options that have already been explained.
- The Appendix contains a list of books that have won the Caldecott Award (as of 2012) and that work well with these activities. Teachers should feel free to use their own books if they already have appropriate resources.
- The on-level menu ● gives students the opportunity to create a commercial. Although students enjoy producing their own videos, there are often difficulties obtaining the equipment and scheduling the use of a video recorder. This activity can be modified by allowing students to act out the commercial (like a play) or, if students have the technology, allowing them to produce a webcam version of their commercial.
- These menus ask students to use recycled materials to create their puppets. This does not mean only plastic and paper; instead, students should focus on using materials in new ways. It works well if a box is started for "recycled" contributions at the beginning of the school year. That way, students always have access to these types of materials.

Time Frame

- 1–2 weeks—Students are given a menu as the unit is started. As the unit progresses throughout the week, students should refer back to the menu options associated with that content. The teacher will go over all of the options for that content and have students circle the items that represent the activities they are most interested in completing. As teaching continues over the next 1–2 weeks, shapes will be colored in as each activity is completed. The activities should be completed in such a way that students complete one from each shape group. When students complete this pattern, they will have completed one activity from each content area, learning style, or level of Bloom's revised taxonomy, depending on the design of the menu.

- 1–2 days—The teacher chooses an activity or product from an objective to use with the entire class during that lesson time.

Suggested Forms

- All-purpose rubric
- Appropriate story map
- Free-choice proposal form (if appropriate for content and level of students)

CALDECOTT WINNERS

Directions: Pick a square. Circle it. Color in the square when you are done.

The Caldecott Medal 	7 Caldecott books I like best 	Caldecott library books 

Directions: Pick a circle. Circle it. Color in the circle when you are done.

Caldecott books on each side

6 Caldecott books

My favorite Caldecott book

Directions: Pick a diamond. Circle it. Color in the diamond when you are done.

Characters from my book

A wordless Caldecott winner

Congratulations on your award!

CALDECOTT WINNERS

Directions: Pick a square. Circle it. Color in the square when you are done.

Make a **poster** to explain the Caldecott Medal and why a book may receive it. 	Create a **flipbook** showing what makes Caldecott books special. 	Make a **list** of library books that have won the Caldecott Medal. 

Directions: Pick a circle. Circle it. Color in the circle when you are done.

Make a Caldecott **cube** with information about a different book on each side.

Design a **scrapbook** of your favorite Caldecott books with information about each one.

Create a **puppet** out of recycled materials for one of the characters in your book.

Directions: Pick a diamond. Circle it. Color in the diamond when you are done.

Write a **story** to go with one of the wordless Caldecott winners from recent years.

Compare and contrast two Caldecott books using a **Venn diagram.**

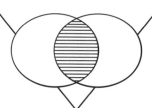

Develop a **commercial** for your favorite illustrated book to convince people that it should win the Caldecott Medal.

CALDECOTT MEDAL CUBE

Directions: Choose 6 different Caldecott Medal books. Place a different book on each side of your **cube**. Include the title, the author's name, and a drawing of the cover. Use this pattern or create your own cube.

 **PARTS OF A BOOK**

GIVE ME 5 MENU

Reading and Communication Objectives Covered Through This Menu and These Activities

- Students will recognize and use different parts of a book.
- Students will use both verbal and nonverbal communication.
- Students will present dramatic interpretations of experiences, stories, poems, and plays.
- Students will clarify and support spoken messages using props.

Writing Objectives Covered Through This Menu and These Activities

- Students will record their knowledge in a variety of ways.
- Students will write to inform, explain, describe, or narrate.

Materials Needed by Students for Completion

- Poster board or large white paper
- Coat hangers (for mobiles) ▲
- String (for mobiles) ▲
- Blank index cards (for concentration cards ● and mobiles ▲)
- Socks (for puppets)
- Paper bags (for puppets)
- Recycled materials (for puppets)

Special Notes on the Modifications of These Menus

- Because the Give Me 5 menu is a point-based menu, it is easy to modify by changing the point goal for those students for whom a goal of 5 may be too much. Lowering the goal on each menu by 1 (or 2) may be more appropriate for some students. Students can color in the "extra" graphics on the bottom of the menu so that the colored graphics match the original goal of 5 points.

Special Notes on the Use of These Menus

- The lower level menu ▲ is specifically designed for students who are lower level readers or for those with a more limited vocabulary. It is meant to simply remind students of product options that have already been explained.

- These menus ask students to use recycled materials to create their puppets. This does not mean only plastic and paper; instead, students should focus on using materials in new ways. It works well if a box is started for "recycled" contributions at the beginning of the school year. That way, students always have access to these types of materials.

Time Frame

- 1–3 days—Students are given a menu as the unit is started, and the teacher discusses all of the product options on the menu. As the different options are discussed, students color the graphic for each option that represents the activity they are most interested in completing so they meet their goal of 5 points. In this menu, that would imply students complete either two products (a 2-point and a 3-point) or one 5-point product. As students complete products, they will color the corresponding graphics along the bottom of the menu so they can track their progress toward their 5-point goal. As the lessons progress throughout the week, the teacher and students refer back to the menu options associated with the content being taught. The teacher may choose to dedicate a learning center to working on menu products or simply allow students time to work after other work is finished.
- 1 day—The teacher chooses an activity or product from the menu to use with the entire class.

Suggested Forms

- All-purpose rubric

Name:_____ ▲

PARTS OF A BOOK

Directions: Choose activities from the menu below. The activities must total 5. Color or circle the picture next to each choice to show which activities you will complete. Color the books along the bottom as you complete your activities to reach 5! All activities must be completed by _____.

2

 The parts of a book

 The parts of a book

3

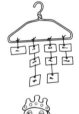 Using different parts of a book

 Mr. Book talking about himself

5

 Finding and using the different parts of a book

 Using all of the parts of a book

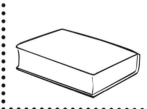 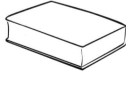 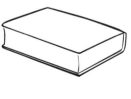  

PARTS OF A BOOK

Directions: Choose activities from the menu below. The activities must total 5. Color or circle the picture next to each choice to show which activities you will complete. Color the books along the bottom as you complete your activities to reach 5! All activities must be completed by _____.

2  Design a **picture dictionary** for all of the different parts of a book.

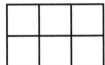 Create a **windowpane** that shows the parts of a book in order from the front to the back.

3 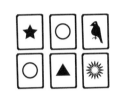 Make a set of **concentration cards** for the different parts of a book and how we use each part.

 Write a **song** that teaches your classmates how to find and use the different parts of a book.

5 Create a book **puppet** to tell your classmates about the different parts of a book.

 Design a **poster** that shows everything a book should have included in it and why each part is important.

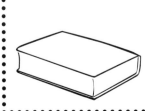 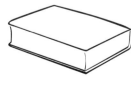 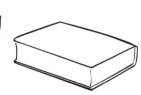 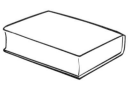 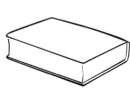

NONFICTION OR INFORMATIONAL TEXT

THREE-SHAPE MENU ▲ AND TIC-TAC-TOE MENU ●

Reading and Communication Objectives Covered Through This Menu and These Activities

- Students will determine meanings of words and develop vocabulary.
- Students will distinguish between fiction and nonfiction.
- Students will use both verbal and nonverbal communication.
- Students will draw illustrations based on text.

Writing Objectives Covered Through This Menu and These Activities

- Students will record their knowledge in a variety of ways.
- Students will write to express their feelings or to reflect.
- Students will write to inform, explain, describe, or narrate.

Materials Needed by Students for Completion

- Poster board or large white paper
- Blank index cards (for trading cards)
- Information Cube template
- Materials for board games (folders, colored cards, etc.)
- Recycled materials (for models)
- Materials for bulletin board displays ●
- Microsoft PowerPoint or other slideshow software ●

Special Notes on the Modifications of These Menus

- This topic has two different menu formats: the Three-Shape menu ▲ and the Tic-Tac-Toe menu ●. The Three-Shape menu is specifically selected for the lower level option as it easily allows the menu to be broken into manageable bits. The menu itself can be cut along the dotted lines into strips of the same shape. Students can then be given the strip of square product choices for their use. Once they have chosen and submitted that product for grading, they can be given the circle strip, and finally the diamond strip. Because this type of menu is designed to become more advanced as students move through the shapes, teachers may choose to provide their lower level students with just the top two shapes and save the diamonds for enrichment.

Special Notes on the Use of These Menus

- The lower level menu ▲ is specifically designed for students who are lower level readers or for those with a more limited vocabulary. It is meant to simply remind students of product options that have already been explained.
- These menus ask students to use recycled materials to create their models. This does not mean only plastic and paper; instead, students should focus on using materials in new ways. It works well if a box is started for "recycled" contributions at the beginning of the school year. That way, students always have access to these types of materials.
- The on-level menu ● allows students to create a bulletin board display. Some classrooms may have only one bulletin board, so the teacher can divide the board into sections, or additional classroom wall or hall space can be sectioned off for the creation of these displays. Students can plan their displays based on the amount of space they are assigned.

Time Frame

- 1–2 weeks—Students are given a menu as the unit is started. As the teacher presents lessons throughout the week, he or she should refer back to the menu options associated with that content. The teacher will go over all of the options for that content and have students select the activities they are most interested in completing. As teaching continues over the next week, activities are completed. For those students working on the Tic-Tac-Toe menu ●, the selected activities should make a column or row. The teacher may choose to dedicate a learning center to working on menu products or simply allow students time to work after other work is finished. When students complete this pattern, they will have completed one activity from each content area, learning style, or level of Bloom's revised taxonomy, depending on the design of the menu.
- 1 week—At the start of the unit, the teacher chooses the three activities he or she feels are most valuable for students. Stations can be set up in the classroom. These three activities are available for student choice throughout the week as regular instruction takes place.

- 1–2 days—The teacher chooses an activity from the menu to use with the entire class.
- 1–2 weeks—Students are given a menu as the unit is started. As the teacher presents lessons throughout the week, he or she should refer back to the menu options associated with that content. The teacher will go over all of the options for that content and have students select the activities they are most interested in completing. As teaching continues over the next week, activities are completed. For those students working on the Tic-Tac-Toe menu ●, the selected activities should make a column or row. The teacher may choose to dedicate a learning center to working on menu products or simply allow students time to work after other work is finished. When students complete this pattern, they will have completed one activity from each content area, learning style, or level of Bloom's revised taxonomy, depending on the design of the menu.
- 1 week—At the start of the unit, the teacher chooses the three activities he or she feels are most valuable for students. Stations can be set up in the classroom. These three activities are available for student choice throughout the week as regular instruction takes place.
- 1–2 days—The teacher chooses an activity from the menu to use with the entire class.

Suggested Forms

- All-purpose rubric

Name:_____ ▲

NONFICTION OR INFORMATIONAL TEXT

Directions: Pick a square. Circle it. Color in the square when you are done.

What I learned	Teaching others about my topic	Three facts

✂ -

Directions: Pick a circle. Circle it. Color in the circle when you are done.

Information from my book

Important words from my book

Questions I still have

✂ -

Directions: Pick a diamond. Circle it. Color in the diamond when you are done.

An example

Questions about my topic

2 things in my book

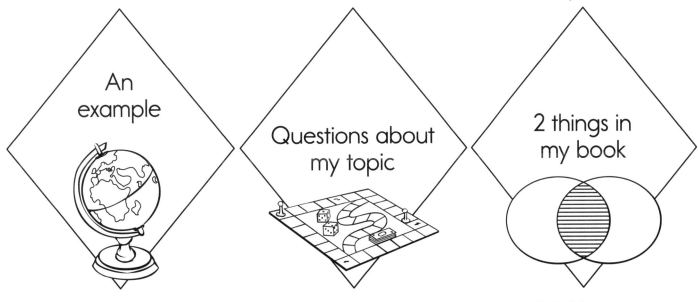

Name:_____ ●

NONFICTION OR INFORMATIONAL TEXT

Directions: Check the boxes you plan to complete. They should form a tic-tac-toe across or down. All activities must be completed by _____.

☐ **Find the Information** Create a set of **trading cards** for information found in your book. 	☐ **Cube It** Complete an information **cube** with information you learned from your book. 	☐ **Compare Information** Compare and contrast two things you read about in your book using a **Venn diagram.** 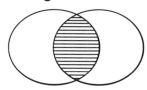
☐ **Sing About It** Sing a **song** to teach others about the information in your book. 	☐ **Questions You Have** Make a **list** of questions you still have about the topic of your book. 	☐ **Share the Information** Make a **bulletin board display** to tell others about the most important information from your book.
☐ **Power Through It** Design a **PowerPoint presentation** to teach your classmates important information you learned from your book.	☐ **Model Your Information** Using recycled materials, create a **model** for something in your book. Label the important information.	☐ **Play With the Information** Design a **board game** for the information shared in your book. 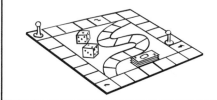

INFORMATION CUBE

Directions: Think of 6 things you learned from your book that you did not know before you read it. Answer the prompts on each side of the **cube**. Use this pattern or create your own cube.

Write the title and author of your book.

Name something you read that you would like to know more about.

Write a fact that you will share with others.

Name an interesting fact that you did not know before you read this book.

Name the most interesting new information you learned.

Name another book on this topic.

 **ALPHABET BOOKS**

GIVE ME 5 MENU ▲
AND 2-5-8 MENU ●

Reading and Communication Objectives Covered Through This Menu and These Activities

- Students will name and identify each letter of the alphabet.
- Students will determine meanings of words and develop vocabulary.
- Students will use both verbal and nonverbal communication.
- Students will present dramatic interpretations of experiences, stories, poems, and plays.
- Students will use and practice alphabetical order.

Writing Objectives Covered Through This Menu and These Activities

- Students will record their knowledge in a variety of ways.
- Students will write to inform, explain, describe, or narrate.

Materials Needed by Students for Completion

- Blank index cards (for trading cards)
- Large blank or lined index cards (for instruction cards) ●
- Socks (for puppets)
- Paper bags (for puppets)
- Recycled materials (for puppets)
- Microsoft PowerPoint or other slideshow software ●
- Alphabet Books Jigsaw Puzzle template ●
- Box (for mystery object) ▲

Special Notes on the Modifications of These Menus

- This topic includes two different types of menus: the Give Me 5 menu ▲ and the 2-5-8 menu ●. Although the primary modification on these two menus is the difference in point goal (5 ▲ vs. 10 ●), further modifications can be made based on the needs of your students. It is easy to modify each menu by simply changing the point goal; lowering the goal on each menu by 1 (or 2) may be more appropriate for some students. Students can color in the "extra" graphics on the bottom of the menu so that the colored graphics match the original goal of 5 or 10 points.

Special Notes on the Use of These Menus

- The lower level menu ▲ is specifically designed for students who are lower level readers or for those with a more limited vocabulary. It is meant to simply remind students of product options that have already been explained.
- The Appendix contains a list of various alphabet books that work well with these activities. Teachers should feel free to use their own if they already have appropriate resources.
- These menus ask students to use recycled materials to create their puppets. This does not mean only plastic and paper; instead, students should focus on using materials in new ways. It works well if a box is started for "recycled" contributions at the beginning of the school year. That way, students always have access to these types of materials.

Time Frame

- 1 week—Students are given a menu as the unit is started, and the teacher discusses all of the product options on the menu. As the different options are discussed, students color or circle the graphic for each option that represents the activity they are most interested in completing so they meet their goal of 5 points (if using the Give Me 5 menu) or 10 points (if using the 2-5-8 menu). As students complete their products, they will color the corresponding graphics along the bottom of the menu so they can track their progress toward their point goal. As the lessons progress through the week, the teacher and students refer back to the menu options associated with the content being taught.
- 1–2 days—The teacher chooses an activity or product from the menu to use with the entire class.

Suggested Forms

- All-purpose rubric
- Free-choice proposal form (if appropriate for content and level of students) ●

ALPHABET BOOKS

Directions: Choose activities from the menu below. The activities must total 5. Color or circle the picture next to each choice to show which activities you will complete. Color the letters along the bottom as you complete your activities to reach 5! All activities must be completed by _____.

2  Words from my book

 Object from my book

3  An ABC puppet

 My alphabet book

5  An ABC book about a science topic

 My own alphabet list with pictures

A B C D E

ALPHABET BOOKS

Directions: Choose activities from the menu below. The activities must total 10 points. Color or circle the picture next to each box to show which activities you will complete. Color the letters along the bottom as you complete your activities to reach 10! All activities must be completed by _____.

2 Points

Turn the letters from your alphabet book into a set of **trading cards**.

Turn your alphabet book into a **jigsaw puzzle** with 6 pieces.

5 Points

After reading your book, design a **puppet** related to the book out of recycled materials.

Write an alphabet **song** about the information in your alphabet book.

Make an **instruction card** to explain how to write a complete alphabet book.

Free choice—Submit a proposal form to your teacher for a product of your choice.

8 Points

Create an alphabet **children's book** about your favorite science topic.

Design an alphabet **PowerPoint presentation** about alphabet books.

A B C D E F G H I J

ALPHABET BOOKS JIGSAW PUZZLE

Directions: Write 6 letters and information from your book on the puzzle pieces. When the puzzle is put together, the letters should be in alphabetical order. You may use this pattern or create your own jigsaw puzzle pieces.

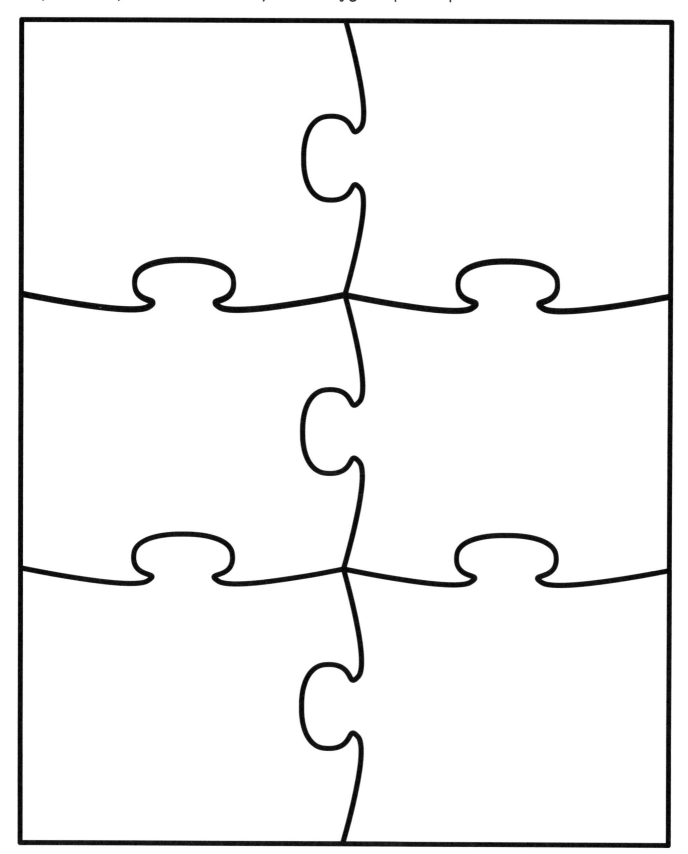

MY CHAPTER BOOK

MEAL MENU

Reading and Communication Objectives Covered Through This Menu and These Activities

- Students will determine meanings of words and develop vocabulary.
- Students will make inferences from reading.
- Students will show comprehension by retelling or acting out events in a story.
- Students will understand story structure through story maps.
- Students will draw illustrations based on text.
- Students will analyze characters, their relationships, and their importance in the story.
- Students will show comprehension by summarizing a story.
- Students will recognize and analyze story plot and problem resolution.

Writing Objectives Covered Through This Menu and These Activities

- Students will write to record their ideas and reflections.
- Students will record their knowledge in a variety of ways.
- Students will write to express their feelings or to reflect.
- Students will write to inform, explain, describe, or narrate.

Materials Needed by Students for Completion

- Poster board or large white paper
- Blank index cards (for mobiles) ▲
- Coat hangers (for mobiles) ▲
- String (for mobiles) ▲
- Magazines (for advertisements and collages ●)
- Blank index cards (for concentration cards and trading cards ▲)
- Character Cube template
- Recycled materials (for dioramas)
- Shoeboxes (for dioramas)
- Box (for mystery object)
- Graph paper or Internet access (for crossword puzzles) ●

Special Notes on the Modifications of These Menus

- The Meal menu format has a design feature that makes it easy to reduce the number of choices students face at one time. Students can be given the left side (breakfast and lunch, or lower levels of thinking) as their first options. After these two meal products have been completed, students can then receive the right side (dinner and dessert, or higher levels of thinking and enrichment options). After becoming accustomed to the amount of choice, students can then get the entire meal menu at once.

Special Notes on the Use of These Menus

- The lower level menu ▲ is specifically designed for students who are lower level readers or for those with a more limited vocabulary. It is meant to simply remind students of product options that have already been explained.
- These menus ask students to use recycled materials to create their dioramas. This does not mean only plastic and paper; instead, students should focus on using materials in new ways. It works well if a box is started for "recycled" contributions at the beginning of the school year. That way, students always have access to these types of materials.

Time Frame

- 1 week—Students are given a menu as the unit is started. As the unit progresses throughout the week, students should refer back to the menu options associated with that content. The teacher will go over all of the options for that content and have students color or circle the graphic for each option that represents the activity they are most interested in completing. As teaching continues, the activities chosen and completed should create a full day's meal, with a breakfast, a lunch, a dinner, and an optional dessert. The teacher may choose to dedicate a learning center to working on menu products or simply allow students time to work after other work is finished. When students complete the menu with this expectation, they have completed one activity from each content area, learning style, or level of Bloom's revised taxonomy, depending on the design of the menu.
- 1–2 days—The teacher chooses an activity or product from an objective to use with the entire class during that lesson time.

Suggested Forms

- All-purpose rubric
- Free-choice proposal form (if appropriate for content and level of students) ●
- Appropriate story map

Name:_____ ▲

MY CHAPTER BOOK

Directions: Choose one activity for breakfast and lunch.

Breakfast

 Vocabulary words from my book

 Important words in my book

 My word

Lunch

 Matching characters to their drawings

 All of my characters

 My favorite character

Directions: Choose one activity for dinner. After you are done with your dinner, you may do a dessert.

Dinner

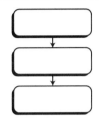

My book

My favorite scene

My book is the best!

Dessert

Another chapter for my book

A card one of the characters could have given another character

Pick a product!

MY CHAPTER BOOK

Directions: Choose one activity for breakfast and lunch.

Breakfast

Create a **picture dictionary** for at least 6 vocabulary words found in your book.

Use 6 vocabulary words from your book in a **song**.

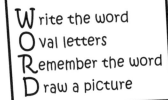

Choose a word you learned in your book and make an **acrostic** for it.

Lunch

Make a set of **concentration cards** to match characters with a drawing you have made of each.

Create a **collage** of pictures that would represent the main character in your book. Label each picture to tell how it relates to that person.

Create a **cube** for one of the characters in your book.

Directions: Choose one activity for dinner. After you are done with your dinner, you may do a dessert.

Dinner

 Complete a **story map** for your book.

 Using recycled materials, create a **diorama** of your favorite scene in the book.

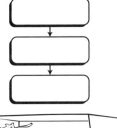

Nice, White Shirt

Create a poster-size **advertisement** for your book that could be used in a bookstore.

Dessert

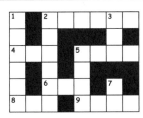 Make a **crossword puzzle** about your book.

 Create a **greeting card** one of your characters could have given another character.

 **Free choice**—Submit a proposal form to your teacher for a product of your choice.

CHARACTER CUBE

Directions: Answer the prompts about your character on each side of the **cube**. Use this pattern or create your own cube.

Name your character.

Draw a picture of your character.

Choose 3 words to describe your character.

Record your favorite thing that your character did.

Record your favorite thing that your character said.

Name one thing you did not like about your character.

 **FABLES**

GIVE ME 5 MENU ▲
AND 2-5-8 MENU ●

Reading and Communication Objectives Covered Through This Menu and These Activities

- Students will show comprehension by retelling or acting out events in a story.
- Students will understand story structure through story maps.
- Students will compare and contrast one literary work with another.
- Students will analyze characters, their relationships, and their importance in the story.
- Students will show comprehension by summarizing a story.
- Students will recognize and analyze story plot and problem resolution.

Writing Objectives Covered Through This Menu and These Activities

- Students will generate ideas before writing.
- Students will write to express their feelings or to reflect.
- Students will write to inform, explain, describe, or narrate.

Materials Needed by Students for Completion

- Poster board or large white paper
- Blank index cards (for mobiles) ●
- String (for mobiles) ●
- Recycled materials (for dioramas) ▲
- Shoeboxes (for dioramas) ▲
- Coat hangers (for mobiles) ●
- Materials for board games

Special Notes on the Modifications of These Menus

- This topic includes two different types of menus: the Give Me 5 menu ▲ and the 2-5-8 menu ●. Although the primary modification on these two menus is the difference in point goal (5 ▲ vs. 10 ●), further modifications can be made based on the needs of your students. It is easy to modify each menu by simply changing the point goal; lowering the goal on each menu by 1 (or 2) may be more appropriate for some students. Students can color in the "extra" graphics on the bottom of the menu so that the colored graphics match the original goal of 5 or 10 points.

Special Notes on the Use of These Menus

- The lower level menu ▲ is specifically designed for students who are lower level readers or for those with a more limited vocabulary. It is meant to simply remind students of product options that have already been explained.
- The lower level menu ▲ asks students to use recycled materials to create their dioramas. This does not mean only plastic and paper; instead, students should focus on using materials in new ways. It works well if a box is started for "recycled" contributions at the beginning of the school year. That way, students always have access to these types of materials.

Time Frame

- 1 week—Students are given a menu as the unit is started, and the teacher discusses all of the product options on the menu. As the different options are discussed, students color or circle the graphic for each option that represents the activity they are most interested in completing so they meet their goal of 5 points (if using the Give Me 5 menu) or 10 points (if using the 2-5-8 menu). As students complete their products, they will color the corresponding graphics along the bottom of the menu so they can track their progress toward their point goal. As the lessons progress through the week, the teacher and students refer back to the menu options associated with the content being taught.
- 1–2 days—The teacher chooses an activity or product from the menu to use with the entire class.

Suggested Forms

- All-purpose rubric
- Free-choice proposal form (if appropriate for content and level of students) ●
- Appropriate story map

Name:_____ ▲

FABLES

Directions: Choose activities from the menu below. The activities must total 5. Color or circle the picture next to each choice to show which activities you will complete. Color the books along the bottom as you complete your activities to reach 5! All activities must be completed by _____.

2  The characters in my fable

The most important character in my fable

3  An important scene in my fable

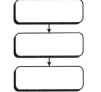 My fable

5  A new ending for my fable

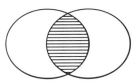 2 different versions of the same fable

 Characters and questions from my fable

   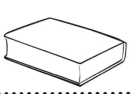 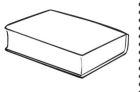

Name:_____ ●

FABLES

Directions: Choose activities from the menu below. The activities must total 10 points. Color or circle the picture next to each box to show which activities you will complete. Color the books along the bottom as you complete your activities to reach 10! All activities must be completed by _____.

2 Points

Create a **mural** showing an important scene from your fable.

Design a **mobile** to show what happens in your fable.

5 Points

Complete a **story map** for your fable.

Use a **Venn diagram** to compare and contrast two different versions of the same fable.

Create a **board game** using characters and questions from your fable.

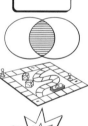

Free choice—Submit a proposal form to your teacher for a product of your choice.

8 Points

Choose your favorite fable. Write a new ending for the **story** with a new moral.

Write a **play** in which humans take on animal traits. Be sure to include a moral and the story map you used to help you write your fable.

GIVE ME 5

FOLK TALES

GIVE ME 5 MENU ▲
AND 2-5-8 MENU ●

Reading and Communication Objectives Covered Through This Menu and These Activities

- Students will show comprehension by retelling or acting out events in a story.
- Students will understand story structure through story maps.
- Students will analyze characters, their relationships, and their importance in the story.
- Students will show comprehension by summarizing a story.
- Students will recognize and analyze story plot and problem resolution.

Writing Objectives Covered Through This Menu and These Activities

- Students will generate ideas before writing.
- Students will write to inform, explain, describe, or narrate.
- Students will write to influence or persuade.

Materials Needed by Students for Completion

- Poster board or large white paper
- Blank index cards (for mobiles) ▲
- Coat hangers (for mobiles) ▲
- String (for mobiles) ▲
- Scrapbooking materials ●
- Recycled materials (for dioramas)
- Shoeboxes (for dioramas)
- Magazines (for advertisements)
- DVD or VHS recorder (for news report) ●

Special Notes on the Modifications of These Menus

- This topic includes two different types of menus: the Give Me 5 menu ▲ and the 2-5-8 menu ●. Although the primary modification on these two menus is the difference in point goal (5 ▲ vs. 10 ●), further modifications can be made based on the needs of your students. It is easy to modify each menu by simply changing the point goal; lowering the goal on each menu by 1 (or 2) may be more appropriate for some students. Students can color in the "extra" graphics on the bottom of the menu so that the colored graphics match the original goal of 5 or 10 points.

Special Notes on the Use of These Menus

- The lower level menu ▲ is specifically designed for students who are lower level readers or for those with a more limited vocabulary. It is meant to simply remind students of product options that have already been explained.
- The Appendix contains a list of various books of fables that work well with these activities. Teachers should feel free to use their own if they already have appropriate resources.
- These menus ask students to use recycled materials to create their dioramas. This does not mean only plastic and paper; instead, students should focus on using materials in new ways. It works well if a box is started for "recycled" contributions at the beginning of the school year. That way, students always have access to these types of materials.
- The on-level menu ● gives students the opportunity to create a news report. Although students enjoy producing their own videos, there are often difficulties obtaining the equipment and scheduling the use of a video recorder. This activity can be modified by allowing students to act out the news report (like a play) or, if students have the technology, allowing them to produce a webcam version of their news report.

Time Frame

- 1 week—Students are given a menu as the unit is started, and the teacher discusses all of the product options on the menu. As the different options are discussed, students color or circle the graphic for each option that represents the activity they are most interested in completing so they meet their goal of 5 points (if using the Give Me 5 menu) or 10 points (if using the 2-5-8 menu). As students complete their products, they will color the corresponding graphics along the bottom of the menu so they can track their progress toward their point goal. As the lessons progress through the week, the teacher and students refer back to the menu options associated with the content being taught.

- 1–2 days—The teacher chooses an activity or product from the menu to use with the entire class.

Suggested Forms

- All-purpose rubric
- Free-choice proposal form (if appropriate for content and level of students) ●
- Appropriate story map

FOLK TALES

Directions: Choose activities from the menu below. The activities must total 5. Color or circle the picture next to each choice to show which activities you will complete. Color the animals along the bottom as you complete your activities to reach 5! All activities must be completed by _____.

2 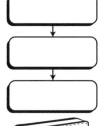 The setting and characters

  One thing about each character

3  My folk tale

 A new book cover

5  My folk tale

 My own folk tale

Name:_____ ●

FOLK TALES

Directions: Choose activities from the menu below. The activities must total 10 points. Color or circle the picture next to each box to show which activities you will complete. Color the animals along the bottom as you complete your activities to reach 10! All activities must be completed by _____.

2 Points

Create a **scrapbook** for your characters' adventures in your folk tale.

Design a **diorama** that shows the setting and characters in your folk tale.

5 Points

Make a **Venn diagram** that compares and contrasts folk tales to fairy tales.

Create an **advertisement** to convince others to learn the lesson taught in your folk tale.

Complete a **story map** for your folk tale.

Free choice—Submit a proposal form to your teacher for a product of your choice.

8 Points

Create a **news report** to share the events that occurred in your folk tale.

Write your own folk tale **story**. Include a story map and a rough draft of your ideas.

FAIRY TALES

PICK 3 MENU ▲ AND TARGET-BASED LIST MENU ●

Reading and Communication Objectives Covered Through This Menu and These Activities

- Students will show comprehension by retelling or acting out events in a story.
- Students will understand story structure through story maps.
- Students will draw illustrations based on text.
- Students will compare and contrast one literary work with another.
- Students will analyze characters, their relationships, and their importance in the story.
- Students will show comprehension by summarizing a story.
- Students will recognize and analyze story plot and problem resolution.

Writing Objectives Covered Through This Menu and These Activities

- Students will write to record their ideas and reflections.
- Students will generate ideas before writing.
- Students will write to inform, explain, describe, or narrate.

Materials Needed by Students for Completion

- Poster board or large white paper
- Blank index cards (for mobiles) ▲
- Coat hangers (for mobiles) ▲
- String (for mobiles) ▲
- Socks (for puppets)
- Paper bags (for puppets)
- Recycled materials (for puppets and dioramas)
- Shoeboxes (for dioramas)
- Materials for board games (folders, colored cards, etc.) ▲
- Scrapbooking materials
- DVD or VHS recorder (for news reports)

Special Notes on the Modifications of These Menus

- This topic has two different menu formats: the Pick 3 menu ▲ and the Target-Based List menu ●. Although the activities are similar, some students may be overwhelmed by the design of the Target-Based List menu. The Pick 3 menu visually distinguishes the options separately using boxes and can be modified further by dividing the page into three sections, in which the students select one option from each section.

Special Notes on the Use of These Menus

- The Appendix contains a list of various fairy tale books that work well with these activities. Teachers should feel free to use their own if they already have appropriate resources.
- These menus ask students to use recycled materials to create their puppets and dioramas. This does not mean only plastic and paper; instead, students should focus on using materials in new ways. It works well if a box is started for "recycled" contributions at the beginning of the school year. That way, students always have access to these types of materials.
- These menus give students the opportunity to create a news report. Although students enjoy producing their own videos, there are often difficulties obtaining the equipment and scheduling the use of a video recorder. This activity can be modified by allowing students to act out the news report (like a play) or, if students have the technology, allowing them to produce a webcam version of their news report.

Time Frame

- 1–2 weeks—Students are given a menu as the unit is started and the guidelines and target number of products are discussed. The Target-Based List menu ● has an open blank at the top so teachers can designate their own target values based on time and knowledge of the students. A target number of 3 is a good place to begin, and teachers can adjust this based on student expertise. There is also an opportunity for extra credit if the teacher would like to use another target number. Because these menus cover one topic in depth, the teacher will go over all of the options on the menus and have students circle or place check marks in the boxes next to the activities they are most interested in completing. If students are using the Target-Based List menu ●, teachers will also need to set aside a few moments to sign the agreement at the bottom of the page with each student; this is not necessary with the Pick 3 menu ▲. As instruction continues, activities are completed by students and submitted for grading. The teacher may choose to dedicate a learning center to working on menu products or simply allow students time to work after other work is finished.

- 1–2 days—The teacher chooses an activity or product from an objective to use with the entire class during that lesson time.

Suggested Forms

- All-purpose rubric
- Free-choice proposal form (if appropriate for content and level of students)
- Appropriate story map

FAIRY TALES

Directions: Circle three activities you would like to do. Color in the square after you are finished.

My fairy tale	Characters in my fairy tale	Adventures in my fairy tale

Most important character in my fairy tale

My favorite scene

Most important thing in my fairy tale

My fairy tale

My product

Free

My own fairy tale

Name:_____ ●

FAIRY TALES

Directions:
1. You may complete as many of the activities listed as you can within the time period.
2. You may choose any combination of activities. Your goal is to complete _____ activities.
3. You may be as creative as you like within the guidelines listed below.
4. You must share your plan with your teacher by _____.

Plan to Do	Activity to Complete	Completed
	Complete a **story map** for your fairy tale.	
	Use a **Venn diagram** to compare and contrast two versions of the same fairy tale.	
	Choose an important character (other than the main character) in your fairy tale and make a **puppet** out of recycled materials for that character.	
	Perform a **news report** about the most important thing that happened in your fairy tale.	
	Design a **map** to show all of the important places in your fairy tale.	
	Write at least three **diary** entries for one character in your fairy tale.	
	Create a **scrapbook** to show all of the main character's adventures.	
	Create a **diorama** of your favorite scene from your fairy tale using recycled materials.	
	Write your own fairy tale **story** for children. Include a story map to help you brainstorm ideas.	
	Free choice—Submit a proposal form to your teacher for a product of your choice.	
	Total number of activities you are planning to complete: **Total number of activities completed:**	

I am planning to complete ____ activities.

Teacher's initials _____ Student's signature _____

CHAPTER 6

Book Menus

AMELIA BEDELIA

GIVE ME 5 MENU ▲
AND 2-5-8 MENU ●

Book Synopsis

• Amelia Bedelia is someone who takes instructions quite literally. For example, when she is told to "dust the furniture," she locates dusting powder and sprinkles it all over the living room furniture and floor. When asked to "draw the drapes when the sun comes in," Amelia sits down with a sketchpad and gives it a try. There are many books in the *Amelia Bedelia* series, and this menu is written in such a way that it could be used with any of them.

Reading and Communication Objectives Covered Through This Menu and These Activities

• Students will make predictions based on what is read.
• Students will show comprehension by retelling or acting out events in a story.
• Students will present dramatic interpretations of experiences, stories, poems, and plays.
• Students will understand story structure through story maps.
• Students will analyze characters, their relationships, and their importance in the story.
• Students will show comprehension by summarizing a story.
• Students will recognize and analyze story plot and problem resolution.

Writing Objectives Covered Through This Menu and These Activities

• Students will generate ideas before writing.
• Students will write to inform, explain, describe, or narrate.

Materials Needed by Students for Completion

• *Amelia Bedelia* books by Peggy Parish
• Blank index cards (for mobiles ▲ and trading cards ▲)
• Coat hangers (for mobiles) ▲
• String (for mobiles) ▲
• Recycled materials (for dioramas) ●

- Shoeboxes (for dioramas) ●
- Scrapbooking materials
- Magazines (for advertisements)
- DVD or VHS recorder (for news report) ●

Special Notes on the Modifications of These Menus

- This topic includes two different types of menus: the Give Me 5 menu ▲ and the 2-5-8 menu ●. Although the primary modification on these two menus is the difference in point goal (5 ▲ vs. 10 ●), further modifications can be made based on the needs of your students. It is easy to modify each menu by simply changing the point goal; lowering the goal on each menu by 1 (or 2) may be more appropriate for some students. Students can color in the "extra" graphics on the bottom of the menu so that the colored graphics match the original goal of 5 or 10 points.

Special Notes on the Use of These Menus

- The lower level menu ▲ is specifically designed for students who are lower level readers or for those with a more limited vocabulary. It is meant to simply remind students of product options that have already been explained.
- The on-level menu ● gives students the opportunity to create a news report. Although students enjoy producing their own videos, there are often difficulties obtaining the equipment and scheduling the use of a video recorder. This activity can be modified by allowing students to act out the news report (like a play) or, if students have the technology, allowing them to produce a webcam version of their news report.
- The on-level menu ● asks students to use recycled materials to create their dioramas. This does not mean only plastic and paper; instead, students should focus on using materials in new ways. It works well if a box is started for "recycled" contributions at the beginning of the school year. That way, students always have access to these types of materials.

Time Frame

- 1 week—Students are given a menu as the unit is started, and the teacher discusses all of the product options on the menu. As the different options are discussed, students color or circle the graphic for each option that represents the activity they are most interested in completing so they meet their goal of 5 points (if using the Give Me 5 menu) or 10 points (if using the 2-5-8 menu). As students complete their products, they will color the corresponding graphics along the bottom of the menu so they can track their progress toward their point goal. As the lessons progress through the week, the teacher and students refer back to the menu options associated with the content being taught.

- 1–2 days—The teacher chooses an activity or product from the menu to use with the entire class.

Suggested Forms

- All-purpose rubric
- Free-choice proposal form (if appropriate for content and level of students) ●
- Appropriate story map

Name:_____ ▲

AMELIA BEDELIA

Directions: Choose activities from the menu below. The activities must total 5. Color or circle the picture next to each choice to show which activities you will complete. Color the brooms along the bottom as you complete your activities to reach 5! All activities must be completed by _____.

2  Amelia Bedelia's actions

 Amelia Bedelia's skills

3  Hire Amelia Bedelia!

 Amelia's Bedelia's job

5  Confusing magazine ads

 Amelia Bedelia's next job

AMELIA BEDELIA

Directions: Choose activities from the menu below. The activities must total 10 points. Color or circle the picture next to each box to show which activities you will complete. Color the brooms along the bottom as you complete your activities to reach 10! All activities must be completed by _____.

2 Points

Make a **diorama** showing your favorite scene in the book.

Create a **picture dictionary** to help people understand Amelia.

5 Points

Create a **scrapbook** of magazine advertisements that may confuse Amelia. Explain what she may do instead.

Design an **advertisement** for Amelia Bedelia's special services.

Amelia Bedelia has made another mistake! Prepare a **news report** to share what has happened this time.

Free choice—Submit a proposal form to your teacher for a product of your choice.

8 Points

Create your own **children's book** about Amelia and her mishaps. Include the story map you used to write your book.

Perform a **play** about what happens to Amelia when she takes her next job.

FROG AND TOAD ARE FRIENDS

THREE-SHAPE MENU ▲ AND TIC-TAC-TOE MENU ●

Book Synopsis

- In this chapter book, Frog and Toad have many adventures, from helping find a lost button to caring for a sick friend. The book introduces the concept of friendship and focuses on its value.

Reading and Communication Objectives Covered Through This Menu and These Activities

- Students will distinguish between fiction and nonfiction.
- Students will compare and contrast their life experiences with those found in readings.
- Students will show comprehension by retelling or acting out events in a story.
- Students will analyze characters, their relationships, and their importance in the story.
- Students will show comprehension by summarizing a story.
- Students will recognize and analyze story plot and problem resolution.

Writing Objectives Covered Through This Menu and These Activities

- Students will write to express their feelings or to reflect.
- Students will write to inform, explain, describe, or narrate.
- Students will write to influence or persuade.

Materials Needed by Students for Completion

- *Frog and Toad Are Friends* by Arnold Lobel
- Poster board or large white paper
- Blank index cards (for trading cards)
- Magazines (for collages and advertisements)
- Scrapbooking materials
- Paper bags (for puppets) ▲
- Socks (for puppets) ▲
- Recycled materials (for puppets) ▲

- Microsoft PowerPoint or other slideshow software ●
- Friendship Cube template ●

Special Notes on the Modifications of These Menus

- This topic has two different menu formats: the Three-Shape menu ▲ and the Tic-Tac-Toe menu ●. The Three-Shape menu is specifically selected for the lower level option as it easily allows the menu to be broken into manageable bits. The menu itself can be cut along the dotted lines into strips of the same shape. Students can then be given the strip of square product choices for their use. Once they have chosen and submitted that product for grading, they can be given the circle strip, and finally the diamond strip. Because this type of menu is designed to become more advanced as students move through the shapes, teachers may choose to provide their lower level students with just the top two shapes and save the diamonds for enrichment.

Special Notes on the Use of These Menus

- The lower level menu ▲ is specifically designed for students who are lower level readers or for those with a more limited vocabulary. It is meant to simply remind students of product options that have already been explained.

Time Frame

- 1–2 weeks—Students are given a menu as the unit is started. As the teacher presents lessons throughout the week, he or she should refer back to the menu options associated with that content. The teacher will go over all of the options for that content and have students select the activities they are most interested in completing. As teaching continues over the next week, activities are completed. For those students working on the Tic-Tac-Toe menu ●, the selected activities should make a column or row. The teacher may choose to dedicate a learning center to working on menu products or simply allow students time to work after other work is finished. When students complete this pattern, they will have completed one activity from each content area, learning style, or level of Bloom's revised taxonomy, depending on the design of the menu.
- 1 week—At the start of the unit, the teacher chooses the three activities he or she feels are most valuable for students. Stations can be set

up in the classroom. These three activities are available for student choice throughout the week as regular instruction takes place.
- 1–2 days—The teacher chooses an activity from the menu to use with the entire class.

Suggested Forms
- All-purpose rubric
- Appropriate story map

Name:_____ ▲

FROG AND TOAD ARE FRIENDS

Directions: Pick a square. Circle it. Color in the square when you are done.

Help find Toad's button	Frog and Toad's summer adventures	Get well soon Frog!

✂ -

Directions: Pick a circle. Circle it. Color in the circle when you are done.

A good friend

I am a good friend!

Being a good friend to everyone

✂ -

Directions: Pick a diamond. Circle it. Color in the diamond when you are done.

Different kinds of frogs and toads

All about frogs and toads

Families of frogs and toads

Name:_____

FROG AND TOAD ARE FRIENDS

Directions: Check the boxes you plan to complete. They should form a tic-tac-toe across or down. All activities must be completed by _____.

☐ **Friendship** Create a **collage** of words and pictures that shows qualities of a good friend. 	☐ **Frog and Toad's Adventures** Design a **scrapbook** about Frog and Toad's summer adventures. 	☐ **Frogs and Toads** Make a **Venn diagram** to compare and contrast frogs and toads. 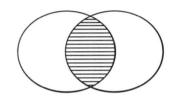
☐ **Frogs and Toads** Create a **PowerPoint presentation** with pictures and facts about frogs and toads. 	☐ **Friendship** Create a friendship **cube** that shows how to be a good friend. 	☐ **Frog and Toad's Adventures** Create a lost and found **advertisement** to help find Toad's button. 
☐ **Frog and Toad's Adventures** Design a **greeting card** Toad may have given Frog when he did not feel well. 	☐ **Frogs and Toads** Create a set of **trading cards** for different kinds of frogs and toads. 	☐ **Friendship** Everyone can be a good friend. Perform a **play** to teach others how to be good friends. 

FRIENDSHIP CUBE

Directions: Think about the qualities of a good friend and write ideas on each side of your **cube** using the prompts. Use this pattern or create your own cube.

List one thing a good friend does.

List 2 words to describe a good friend.

Share one thing a good friend says.

Draw a good friend.

Share one thing you would tell a good friend.

How do you know if a friend is a good friend?

THE RAINBOW FISH

THREE-SHAPE MENU

Book Synopsis

- Rainbow Fish is the most beautiful fish in the ocean because of his beautiful sparkling silver scales. Unfortunately, Rainbow Fish does not have any friends, and when he hurts the feeling of one of his many admirers, the other fish in the ocean decide to ignore him. After some advice from a wise octopus, he has to decide whether his beauty is more important than having friends.

Reading and Communication Objectives Covered Through This Menu and These Activities

- Students will show comprehension by retelling or acting out events in a story.
- Students will present dramatic interpretations of experiences, stories, poems, and plays.
- Students will understand story structure through story maps.
- Students will analyze characters, their relationships, and their importance in the story.
- Students will show comprehension by summarizing a story.
- Students will recognize and analyze story plot and problem resolution.

Writing Objectives Covered Through This Menu and These Activities

- Students will write to inform, explain, describe, or narrate.
- Students will write to influence or persuade.

Materials Needed by Students for Completion

- *The Rainbow Fish* by Marcus Pfister
- Poster board or large white paper
- Socks (for puppets) ▲
- Paper bags (for puppets) ▲
- Recycled materials (for puppets ▲ and models ●)
- Blank index cards (for mobiles)
- Coat hangers (for mobiles)
- String (for mobiles)

- Magazines (for advertisements)
- Ruler (for comic strip) ●
- Materials for board games ▲

Special Notes on the Modifications of These Menus

- These two Three-Shape menus have slightly different formats. The lower level menu ▲ has a dotted line with separate instructions for each section. This visually separates the page beyond just the different shapes. This also makes it easy for the teacher to cut the menu as needed based on the comfort level of the students when it comes to choice. If it is the first time choice is being introduced, the children may receive only the strip of square options. Then when they have finished, they can receive the circles and then the diamonds. After students are more accustomed to options, the menu might be cut just once after the circles, so students can select a square and a circle and submit them to the teacher. Then they can choose from the diamond strip they receive. The ultimate goal would be to work up to allowing students to have all nine options at once and not be overwhelmed. The on-level menu ● has one dotted line separating the diamonds from the rest of the menu, making the enrichment options easy to include or cut and distribute later at the teacher's discretion.

Special Notes on the Use of These Menus

- The lower level menu ▲ is specifically designed for students who are lower level readers or for those with a more limited vocabulary. It is meant to simply remind students of product options that have already been explained.
- These menus ask students to use recycled materials to create their puppets and models. This does not mean only plastic and paper; instead, students should focus on using materials in new ways. It works well if a box is started for "recycled" contributions at the beginning of the school year. That way, students always have access to these types of materials.

Time Frame

- 1–2 weeks—Students are given a menu as the unit is started. As the unit progresses throughout the week, students should refer back to the menu options associated with that content. The teacher will go over all of the options for that content and have students circle the items that represent the activities they are most interested in completing. As teaching continues over the next 1–2 weeks, shapes will be colored in as each activity is completed. The activities should be completed in such a way that students complete one from each shape group. When students complete this pattern, they will have completed one activity from each content area, learning style, or level of Bloom's revised taxonomy, depending on the design of the menu.

- 1–2 days—The teacher chooses an activity or product from an objective to use with the entire class during that lesson time.

Suggested Forms

- All-purpose rubric
- Appropriate story map

Name:_____ ▲

THE RAINBOW FISH

Directions: Pick a square. Circle it. Color in the square when you are done.

| Rainbow Fish  | Come to school as Rainbow Fish  | Everyone Rainbow Fish talks to in the story  |

Directions: Pick a circle. Circle it. Color in the circle when you are done.

Rainbow Fish's shiny scales

Information
$8.00
Nice, White Shirt

Giving thanks to the octopus

The Rainbow Fish

Directions: Pick a diamond. Circle it. Color in the diamond when you are done.

Being a good friend

Sharing with others

Why friends are important

THE RAINBOW FISH

Directions: Pick a square. Circle it. Color in the square when you are done.

Design a **model** of Rainbow Fish using recycled materials.

Come to school as Rainbow Fish and share all day long.

Develop a **mobile** of all of the fish that Rainbow Fish talks to in the book.

Directions: Pick a circle. Circle it. Color in the circle when you are done.

Create an **advertisement** for Rainbow Fish's shiny scales.

Information
$8.00
Nice, White Shirt

Make a thank-you **greeting card** that Rainbow Fish might give the octopus at the end of the story.

Complete **a story map** for *The Rainbow Fish.*

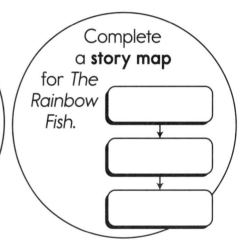

Directions: Pick a diamond. Circle it. Color in the diamond when you are done.

Make a **comic strip** that shows why sharing is important.

Create a **class game** to show what people can do to be good friends.

Sing your own **song** about why you should share.

PICK 3   DR. SEUSS

PICK 3 MENU ▲ AND
TARGET-BASED LIST MENU ●

Reading and Communication Objectives Covered Through This Menu and These Activities

- Students will determine meanings of words and develop vocabulary.
- Students will distinguish between fiction and nonfiction.
- Students will show comprehension by retelling or acting out events in a story.
- Students will understand story structure through story maps.
- Students will compare and contrast one literary work with another. ●
- Students will show comprehension by summarizing a story.
- Students will recognize and analyze story plot and problem resolution.

Writing Objectives Covered Through This Menu and These Activities

- Students will generate ideas before writing.
- Students will write to inform, explain, describe, or narrate.
- Students will write to influence or persuade.

Materials Needed by Students for Completion

- Poster board or large white paper
- Socks (for puppets) ▲
- Paper bags (for puppets) ▲
- Recycled materials (for puppets) ▲
- Blank index cards (for trading cards) ●
- Materials for board games (folders, colored cards, etc.) ●
- Scrapbooking materials ●
- DVD or VHS recorder (for commercials) ●

Special Notes on the Modifications of These Menus

- This topic has two different menu formats: the Pick 3 menu ▲ and the Target-Based List menu ●. Although the activities are similar, some students may be overwhelmed by the design of the Target-Based List menu. The Pick 3 menu visually distinguishes the options separately using boxes and can be modified further by dividing the page into three sections, in which the students select one option from each section.

Special Notes on the Use of These Menus

- There are many Dr. Seuss books available. Books can be selected and assigned based on student reading levels, with the same menu being provided for everyone in the class.
- The lower level menu ▲ asks students to use recycled materials to create their puppets. This does not mean only plastic and paper; instead, students should focus on using materials in new ways. It works well if a box is started for "recycled" contributions at the beginning of the school year. That way, students always have access to these types of materials.

Time Frame

- 1–2 weeks—Students are given a menu as the unit is started and the guidelines and target number of products are discussed. The Target-Based List menu ● has an open blank at the top so teachers can designate their own target values based on time and knowledge of the students. A target number of 3 is a good place to begin, and teachers can adjust this based on student expertise. There is also an opportunity for extra credit if the teacher would like to use another target number. Because these menus cover one topic in depth, the teacher will go over all of the options on the menus and have students circle or place check marks in the boxes next to the activities they are most interested in completing. If students are using the Target-Based List menu ●, teachers will also need to set aside a few moments to sign the agreement at the bottom of the page with each student; this is not necessary with the Pick 3 menu ▲. As instruction continues, activities are completed by students and submitted for grading. The teacher may choose to dedicate a learning center to working on menu products or simply allow students time to work after other work is finished.
- 1–2 days—The teacher chooses an activity or product from an objective to use with the entire class during that lesson time.

Suggested Forms

- All-purpose rubric
- Free-choice proposal form (if appropriate for content and level of students) ●
- Appropriate story map

DR. SEUSS

Directions: Circle three activities you would like to do. Color in the square after you are finished.

All of the things that are not real

Made-up words

DICTIONARY

My favorite character or object

My own story like Dr. Seuss

My Story Book

An invention from my book

All about Dr. Seuss

A new cover for my book

My book

A song one of my characters or objects might sing

DR. SEUSS

Directions:
1. You may complete as many of the activities listed as you can within the time period.
2. You may choose any combination of activities. Your goal is to complete _____ activities.
3. You may be as creative as you like within the guidelines listed below.
4. You must share your plan with your teacher by _____.

Plan to Do	Activity to Complete	Completed
	Make a **list** of all of the things in your book that are not real.	
	Create a **picture dictionary** for the words in your book that were made up.	
	Design a set of **trading cards** for the characters in your story.	
	Compare and contrast two Dr. Seuss books using a **Venn diagram**.	
	Complete a **story map** to share what happened in your book.	
	Using the characters and setting from your book, develop a **board game**.	
	Create a **commercial** for an invention shown in your book.	
	Make a **scrapbook** of the adventures found in your book.	
	Make up a **song** that one of the characters or objects in your book would sing.	
	Write your own creative **story** in the style of Dr. Seuss. Include the completed story map you used to help you write your story.	
	Free choice—Submit a proposal form to your teacher for a product of your choice.	
	Total number of activities you are planning to complete: **Total number of activities completed:**	

I am planning to complete ____ activities.

Teacher's initials _____ Student's signature _____

CHAPTER 7

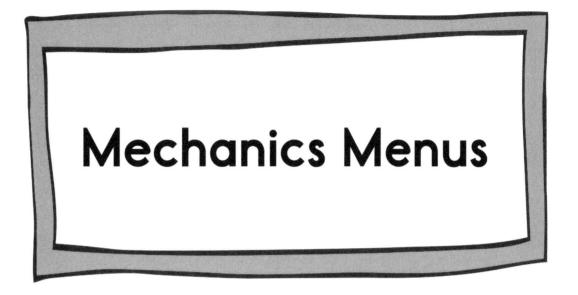

Mechanics Menus

LETTER SOUNDS

THREE-SHAPE MENU

Reading and Communication Objectives Covered Through This Menu and These Activities

- Students will demonstrate print awareness.
- Students will name and identify each letter of the alphabet.
- Students will use both verbal and nonverbal communication.

Writing Objectives Covered Through This Menu and These Activities

- Students will record their knowledge in a variety of ways.

Materials Needed by Students for Completion

- Blank index cards (for concentration cards and games ●)
- Magazines (for collages)
- Socks (for puppets) ●
- Paper bags (for puppets) ●
- Recycled materials (for puppets) ●
- Scrapbooking materials
- Letter Sounds Jigsaw Puzzle template ●
- Box (for mystery object) ▲

Special Notes on the Modifications of These Menus

- These two Three-Shape menus have slightly different formats. The lower level menu ▲ has a dotted line with separate instructions for each section. This visually separates the page beyond just the different shapes. This also makes it easy for the teacher to cut the menu as needed based on the comfort level of the students when it comes to choice. If it is the first time choice is being introduced, the children may receive only the strip of square options. Then when they have finished, they can receive the circles and then the diamonds. After students are more accustomed to options, the menu might be cut just once after the circles, so students can select a square and a circle and submit them to the teacher. Then they can choose from the diamond strip they receive. The ultimate goal would be to work up to allowing students to have all nine options at once and not be overwhelmed. The on-level menu ● has one dotted line separating the diamonds from the rest of the menu, making the enrichment options easy to include or cut and distribute later at the teacher's discretion.

Special Notes on the Use of These Menus

- The lower level menu ▲ is specifically designed for students who are lower level readers or for those with a more limited vocabulary. It is meant to simply remind students of product options that have already been explained.
- The on-level menu ● asks students to use recycled materials to create their puppets. This does not mean only plastic and paper; instead, students should focus on using materials in new ways. It works well if a box is started for "recycled" contributions at the beginning of the school year. That way, students always have access to these types of materials.
- This menu gives students the opportunity to demonstrate a concept. This can take a significant amount of time and organization. It can save time if the demonstration is recorded to share at a later time or if all of the students who choose to do a demonstration sign up for a designated day and time.

Time Frame

- 1–2 weeks—Students are given a menu as the unit is started. As the unit progresses throughout the week, students should refer back to the menu options associated with that content. The teacher will go over all of the options for that content and have students circle the items that represent the activities they are most interested in completing. As teaching continues over the next 1–2 weeks, shapes will be colored in as each activity is completed. The activities should be completed in such a way that students complete one from each shape group. When students complete this pattern, they will have completed one activity from each content area, learning style, or level of Bloom's revised taxonomy, depending on the design of the menu.
- 1–2 days—The teacher chooses an activity or product from an objective to use with the entire class during that lesson time.

Suggested Forms

- All-purpose rubric

Name:_____ ▲

LETTER SOUNDS

Directions: Pick a square. Circle it. Color in the square when you are done.

My first letter sound 	All of the first letter sounds 	5 letter sounds 

Directions: Pick a circle. Circle it. Color in the circle when you are done.

Letter sounds and pictures

Letter sounds and word pictures

My letter sound

Directions: Pick a diamond. Circle it. Color in the diamond when you are done.

Learning letter sounds

Things for each letter sound

First letter sounds with a picture

LETTER SOUNDS

Directions: Pick a square. Circle it. Color in the square when you are done.

Create a **picture dictionary** of first letter sounds with word pictures for each. 	Do a **demonstration** and point out something in the classroom for each initial letter sound. 	Choose a letter sound. Design a **collage** of pictures for your letter sound.

Directions: Pick a circle. Circle it. Color in the circle when you are done.

Make a **scrapbook** of things for each of your letter sounds.

Make a set of **concentration cards** to match letter sounds with word pictures for the sounds.

Which letter sound is used most often? Develop a **jigsaw puzzle** for that sound.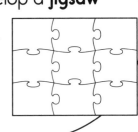

✂ –

Directions: Pick a diamond. Circle it. Color in the diamond when you are done.

Sing a **song** to your classmates to teach different letter sounds.

Design a letter sound card **game**.

Using recycled materials, create a letter **puppet** to explain letter sounds to your classmates.

LETTER SOUNDS JIGSAW PUZZLE

Directions: Draw one thing that has your letter sound on each puzzle piece. When the puzzle is put together, the puzzle should be one complete picture. You may use this pattern or create your own jigsaw puzzle pieces.

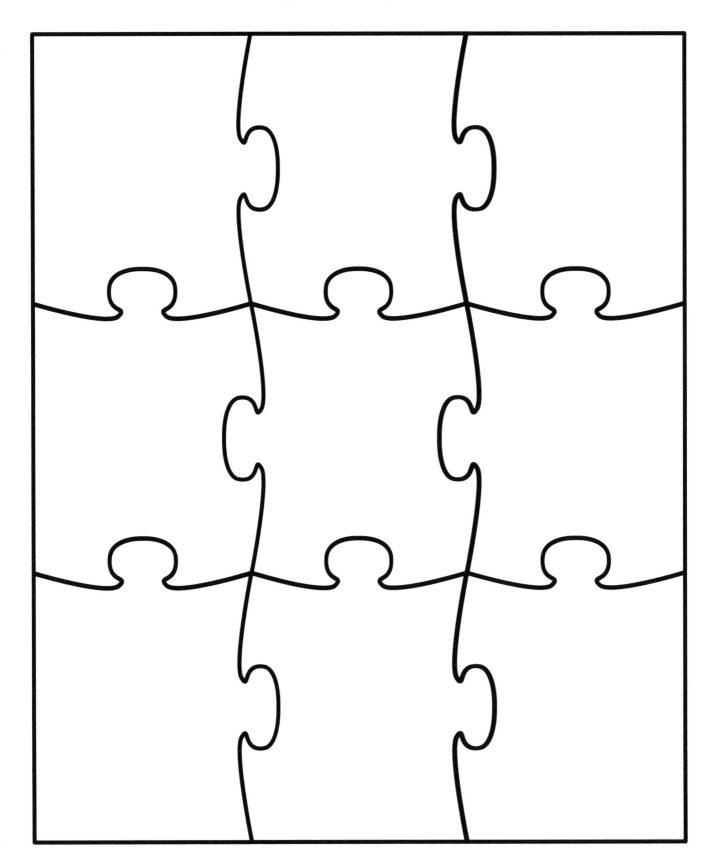

THE ALPHABET

THREE-SHAPE MENU

Reading and Communication Objectives Covered Through This Menu and These Activities

- Students will demonstrate print awareness.
- Students will name and identify each letter of the alphabet.
- Students will determine meanings of words and develop vocabulary.

Writing Objectives Covered Through This Menu and These Activities

- Students will write to record their ideas and reflections.
- Students will record their knowledge in a variety of ways.

Materials Needed by Students for Completion

- Poster board or large white paper
- Blank index cards (for concentration cards)
- Materials for model ▲

Special Notes on the Modifications of These Menus

- These two Three-Shape menus have slightly different formats. The lower level menu ▲ has a dotted line with separate instructions for each section. This visually separates the page beyond just the different shapes. This also makes it easy for the teacher to cut the menu as needed based on the comfort level of the students when it comes to choice. If it is the first time choice is being introduced, the children may receive only the strip of square options. Then when they have finished, they can receive the circles and then the diamonds. After students are more accustomed to options, the menu might be cut just once after the circles, so students can select a square and a circle and submit them to the teacher. Then they can choose from the diamond strip they receive. The ultimate goal would be to work up to allowing students to have all nine options at once and not be overwhelmed. The on-level menu ● has one dotted line separating the diamonds from the rest of the menu, making the enrichment options easy to include or cut and distribute later at the teacher's discretion.

Special Notes on the Use of These Menus

- The lower level menu ▲ is specifically designed for students who are lower level readers or for those with a more limited vocabulary. It is meant to simply remind students of product options that have already been explained.

Time Frame

- 1–2 weeks—Students are given a menu as the unit is started. As the unit progresses throughout the week, students should refer back to the menu options associated with that content. The teacher will go over all of the options for that content and have students circle the items that represent the activities they are most interested in completing. As teaching continues over the next 1–2 weeks, shapes will be colored in as each activity is completed. The activities should be completed in such a way that students complete one from each shape group. When students complete this pattern, they will have completed one activity from each content area, learning style, or level of Bloom's revised taxonomy, depending on the design of the menu.
- 1–2 days—The teacher chooses an activity or product from an objective to use with the entire class during that lesson time.

Suggested Forms

- All-purpose rubric

THE ALPHABET

Directions: Pick a square. Circle it. Color in the square when you are done.

Lowercase and uppercase letters	Lowercase and uppercase letters in order	4 different ways you can sort letters

✂ -

Directions: Pick a circle. Circle it. Color in the circle when you are done.

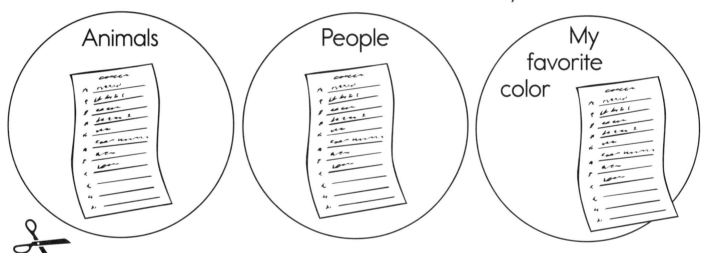

Animals   People   My favorite color

✂ -

Directions: Pick a diamond. Circle it. Color in the diamond when you are done.

Words my letter is in   An alphabet monster   The spelling of my name

THE ALPHABET

Directions: Pick a square. Circle it. Color in the square when you are done.

Design a set of **concentration cards** to match lowercase and uppercase letters. 	**List** the lowercase and uppercase letters of the alphabet in order. 	Create a **poster** to show at least four different ways you can sort or classify letters. 

Directions: Pick a circle. Circle it. Color in the circle when you are done.

Create a **list** of animals using each letter of the alphabet.

Choose your favorite color. Create a **list** of things that are that color, using each letter of the alphabet.

Make a **list** of interesting words using each letter of the alphabet.

Directions: Pick a diamond. Circle it. Color in the diamond when you are done.

Draw of a **map** of your classroom, pointing out all of the things that start with the first letter of your first or last name.

Pretend you are your favorite letter and act out words in which you appear.

Make a **drawing** of a letter on large paper, and add details to change it into a big, unknown creature.

WRITING SENTENCES

GIVE ME 5 MENU

Reading and Communication Objectives Covered Through This Menu and These Activities

- Students will demonstrate print awareness.
- Students will name and identify each letter of the alphabet.
- Students will determine meanings of words and develop vocabulary.

Writing Objectives Covered Through This Menu and These Activities

- Students will record their knowledge in a variety of ways.
- Students will write to express their feelings or to reflect.
- Students will write to inform, explain, describe, or narrate.

Materials Needed by Students for Completion

- Poster board or large white paper
- Blank index cards (for mobiles and concentration cards ●)
- Coat hangers (for mobiles)
- String (for mobiles)

Special Notes on the Modifications of These Menus

- Because the Give Me 5 menu is a point-based menu, it is easy to modify by changing the point goal for those students for whom a goal of 5 may be too much. Lowering the goal on each menu by 1 (or 2) may be more appropriate for some students. Students can color in the "extra" graphics on the bottom of the menu so that the colored graphics match the original goal of 5 points.

Special Notes on the Use of These Menus

- The lower level menu ▲ is specifically designed for students who are lower level readers or for those with a more limited vocabulary. It is meant to simply remind students of product options that have already been explained.

Time Frame

- 1–3 days—Students are given a menu as the unit is started, and the teacher discusses all of the product options on the menu. As the different options are discussed, students color the graphic for each option that represents the activity they are most interested in completing so they meet their goal of 5 points. In this menu, that would imply students complete either two products (a 2-point and a 3-point) or one 5-point product. As students complete products, they will color the corresponding graphics along the bottom of the menu so they can track their progress toward their 5-point goal. As the lessons progress throughout the week, the teacher and students refer back to the menu options associated with the content being taught. The teacher may choose to dedicate a learning center to working on menu products or simply allow students time to work after other work is finished.
- 1 day—The teacher chooses an activity or product from the menu to use with the entire class.

Suggested Forms

- All-purpose rubric

WRITING SENTENCES

Directions: Choose activities from the menu below. The activities must total 5. Color or circle the picture next to each choice to show which activities you will complete. Color the pencils along the bottom as you complete your activities to reach 5! All activities must be completed by _____.

2      A 3-word sentence

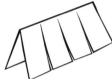   A 4-word sentence

3      3 sentences about me

   4 sentences with pictures

5      My name

   Writing a sentence

Name:_____ ●

WRITING SENTENCES

Directions: Choose activities from the menu below. The activities must total 5. Color or circle the picture next to each choice to show which activities you will complete. Color the pencils along the bottom as you complete your activities to reach 5! All activities must be completed by _____.

2

Write a sentence with at least 3 words and turn it into a **mobile**.

Design a **flipbook** for a simple sentence with 4 flaps. Include a drawing inside.

3

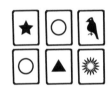

Create a set of sentence **concentration cards**.

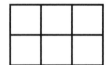

Write 6 sentences in a **windowpane**. Include a picture for each sentence.

5

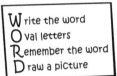

Design an **acrostic** for your name. Use each letter to write a sentence about yourself.

Write a **song** about how to write a sentence and share it with your classmates.

ALPHABETICAL ORDER

THREE-SHAPE MENU

Reading and Communication Objectives Covered Through This Menu and These Activities

- Students will name and identify each letter of the alphabet.
- Students will use and practice alphabetical order.

Writing Objectives Covered Through This Menu and These Activities

- Students will write to record their ideas and reflections.
- Students will record their knowledge in a variety of ways.
- Students will write to express their feelings or to reflect.
- Students will write to inform, explain, describe, or narrate.

Materials Needed by Students for Completion

- Poster board or large white paper
- Large blank or lined index cards (for instruction cards) ●
- Materials for board games
- Magazines (for collages)
- DVD or VHS recorder (for commercials ● and news reports)

Special Notes on the Modifications of These Menus

- These two Three-Shape menus have slightly different formats. The lower level menu ▲ has a dotted line with separate instructions for each section. This visually separates the page beyond just the different shapes. This also makes it easy for the teacher to cut the menu as needed based on the comfort level of the students when it comes to choice. If it is the first time choice is being introduced, the children may receive only the strip of square options. Then when they have finished, they can receive the circles and then the diamonds. After students are more accustomed to options, the menu might be cut just once after the circles, so students can select a square and a circle and submit them to the teacher. Then they can choose from the diamond strip they receive. The ultimate goal would be to work up to allowing students to have all nine options at once and not be overwhelmed. The on-level menu ● has one dotted line separating the diamonds from the rest of the menu, making the enrichment options easy to include or cut and distribute later at the teacher's discretion.

Special Notes on the Use of These Menus

- The lower level menu ▲ is specifically designed for students who are lower level readers or for those with a more limited vocabulary. It is meant to simply remind students of product options that have already been explained.
- These menus give students the opportunity to create a commercial (●) or a news report. Although students enjoy producing their own videos, there are often difficulties obtaining the equipment and scheduling the use of a video recorder. This activity can be modified by allowing students to act out the commercial or news report (like a play) or, if students have the technology, allowing them to produce a webcam version of their commercial or news report.
- This menu gives students the opportunity to demonstrate a concept. This can take a significant amount of time and organization. It can save time if the demonstration is recorded to share at a later time or if all of the students who choose to do a demonstration sign up for a designated day and time.

Time Frame

- 1–2 weeks—Students are given a menu as the unit is started. As the unit progresses throughout the week, students should refer back to the menu options associated with that content. The teacher will go over all of the options for that content and have students circle the items that represent the activities they are most interested in completing. As teaching continues over the next 1–2 weeks, shapes will be colored in as each activity is completed. The activities should be completed in such a way that students complete one from each shape group. When students complete this pattern, they will have completed one activity from each content area, learning style, or level of Bloom's revised taxonomy, depending on the design of the menu.
- 1–2 days—The teacher chooses an activity or product from an objective to use with the entire class during that lesson time.

Suggested Forms

- All-purpose rubric

ALPHABETICAL ORDER

Directions: Pick a square. Circle it. Color in the square when you are done.

Putting words in alphabetical order	How to alphabetize 8 words	Words in alphabetical order

✂ -

Directions: Pick a circle. Circle it. Color in the circle when you are done.

8 new words in alphabetical order	Science vocabulary words	Characters from my story in alphabetical order
	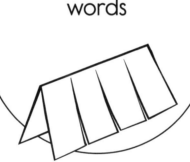	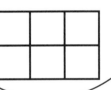

✂ -

Directions: Pick a diamond. Circle it. Color in the diamond when you are done.

Practicing alphabetical order	Someone did not alphabetize!	My ABC book

Name:_____ ●

ALPHABETICAL ORDER

Directions: Pick a square. Circle it. Color in the square when you are done.

Sing a **song** about putting words in alphabetical order. 	Make a **poster** that shows how to alphabetize. 	Design an **instruction card** to show the steps to follow in alphabetizing. 

Directions: Pick a circle. Circle it. Color in the circle when you are done.

List all of the different ways people use alphabetical order.

Make a **flipbook** for your science vocabulary words in alphabetical order.

Design a **windowpane** of the characters from a book you read, listed in alphabetical order.

- -

Directions: Pick a diamond. Circle it. Color in the diamond when you are done.

Why is alphabetical order important? Develop a **commercial** to share this with others.

Prepare a **news report** that discusses a disaster that occurred because someone did not alphabetize.

Ms. Alphabetize believes everything should be alphabetized! Write a **children's book** showing whether this is a good or a bad idea.

 **PUNCTUATION**

GIVE ME 5 MENU

Reading and Communication Objectives Covered Through This Menu and These Activities

- Students will demonstrate use of various forms of punctuation.
- Students will determine meanings of words and develop vocabulary.

Writing Objectives Covered Through This Menu and These Activities

- Students will write to inform, explain, describe, or narrate.
- Students will write to influence or persuade.

Materials Needed by Students for Completion

- Poster board or large white paper
- Blank index cards (for mobiles)
- Coat hangers (for mobiles)
- String (for mobiles)
- Socks (for puppets) ▲
- Paper bags (for puppets) ▲
- Recycled materials (for puppets) ▲
- Large blank or lined index cards (for instruction cards)
- Materials for bulletin board displays ●
- Microsoft PowerPoint or other slideshow software ▲

Special Notes on the Modifications of These Menus

- Because the Give Me 5 menu is a point-based menu, it is easy to modify by changing the point goal for those students for whom a goal of 5 may be too much. Lowering the goal on each menu by 1 (or 2) may be more appropriate for some students. Students can color in the "extra" graphics on the bottom of the menu so that the colored graphics match the original goal of 5 points.

Special Notes on the Use of These Menus

- The lower level menu ▲ is specifically designed for students who are lower level readers or for those with a more limited vocabulary. It is meant to simply remind students of product options that have already been explained.

- These menus ask students to use recycled materials to create their puppets. This does not mean only plastic and paper; instead, students should focus on using materials in new ways. It works well if a box is started for "recycled" contributions at the beginning of the school year. That way, students always have access to these types of materials.
- The on-level menu ● allows students to create a bulletin board display. Some classrooms may have only one bulletin board, so the teacher can divide the board into sections, or additional classroom wall or hall space can be sectioned off for the creation of these displays. Students can plan their displays based on the amount of space they are assigned.

Time Frame

- 1–3 days—Students are given a menu as the unit is started, and the teacher discusses all of the product options on the menu. As the different options are discussed, students color the graphic for each option that represents the activity they are most interested in completing so they meet their goal of 5 points. In this menu, that would imply students complete either two products (a 2-point and a 3-point) or one 5-point product. As students complete products, they will color the corresponding graphics along the bottom of the menu so they can track their progress toward their 5-point goal. As the lessons progress throughout the week, the teacher and students refer back to the menu options associated with the content being taught. The teacher may choose to dedicate a learning center to working on menu products or simply allow students time to work after other work is finished.
- 1 day—The teacher chooses an activity or product from the menu to use with the entire class.

Suggested Forms

- All-purpose rubric

PUNCTUATION

Directions: Choose activities from the menu below. The activities must total 5. Color or circle the picture next to each choice to show which activities you will complete. Color the exclamation points along the bottom as you complete your activities to reach 5! All activities must be completed by _____.

2  Punctuation marks and their use

 Different punctuation marks

3  Using punctuation marks

 Teaching others how to use the different types of punctuation marks

5  Punctuation and using it everyday

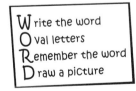 Using only exclamation marks

PUNCTUATION

Directions: Choose activities from the menu below. The activities must total 5. Color or circle the picture next to each choice to show which activities you will complete. Color the exclamation points along the bottom as you complete your activities to reach 5! All activities must be completed by _____.

2

 Make a **mobile** for the punctuation marks being studied with an example of how each is used.

 Create a **picture dictionary** for the different punctuation marks.

3

 Write an **instruction card** to explain how to use punctuation marks. Include examples.

 Create a punctuation **bulletin board display** with explanations and examples.

5

 Create a **folded quiz book** to test your classmates on how to use punctuation marks.

 Write three **journal** entries: one that only uses exclamation marks, one that only uses question marks, and one that only uses periods.

SPELLING

THREE-SHAPE MENU

Reading and Communication Objectives Covered Through This Menu and These Activities

- Students will determine meanings of words and develop vocabulary.
- Students will use and practice alphabetical order.
- Students will use reference materials to build word meanings.

Writing Objectives Covered Through This Menu and These Activities

- Students will write to record their ideas and reflections.
- Students will record their knowledge in a variety of ways.
- Students will write to inform, explain, describe, or narrate.

Materials Needed by Students for Completion

- Poster board or large white paper
- Blank index cards (for concentration cards and mobiles ▲)
- Coat hangers (for mobiles) ▲
- String (for mobiles) ▲
- Magazines (for collages)
- Socks (for puppets)
- Paper bags (for puppets)
- Recycled materials (for puppets)
- Materials for board games ●
- Graph paper or Internet access (for crossword puzzles) ●

Special Notes on the Modifications of These Menus

- These two Three-Shape menus have slightly different formats. The lower level menu ▲ has a dotted line with separate instructions for each section. This visually separates the page beyond just the different shapes. This also makes it easy for the teacher to cut the menu as needed based on the comfort level of the students when it comes to choice. If it is the first time choice is being introduced, the children may receive only the strip of square options. Then when they have finished, they can receive the circles and then the diamonds. After students are more accustomed to options, the menu might be cut just once after the circles, so students can select a square and a circle and submit them to the teacher. Then they can choose from the diamond strip they receive. The ultimate goal would be to work up to allowing students to have all nine options at once and not be overwhelmed. The on-level menu ● has one dotted line separating the diamonds from the rest of the menu, making the enrichment options easy to include or cut and distribute later at the teacher's discretion.

Special Notes on the Use of These Menus

- The lower level menu ▲ is specifically designed for students who are lower level readers or for those with a more limited vocabulary. It is meant to simply remind students of product options that have already been explained.
- These menus ask students to use recycled materials to create their puppets. This does not mean only plastic and paper; instead, students should focus on using materials in new ways. It works well if a box is started for "recycled" contributions at the beginning of the school year. That way, students always have access to these types of materials.

Time Frame

- 1–2 weeks—Students are given a menu as the unit is started. As the unit progresses throughout the week, students should refer back to the menu options associated with that content. The teacher will go over all of the options for that content and have students circle the items that represent the activities they are most interested in completing. As teaching continues over the next 1–2 weeks, shapes will be colored in as each activity is completed. The activities should be completed in such a way that students complete one from each shape group. When students complete this pattern, they will have completed one activity from each content area, learning style, or level of Bloom's revised taxonomy, depending on the design of the menu.
- 1–2 days—The teacher chooses an activity or product from an objective to use with the entire class during that lesson time.

Suggested Forms

- All-purpose rubric

Name:_____ ▲

SPELLING

Directions: Pick a square. Circle it. Color in the square when you are done.

My weekly words	My weekly words in alphabetical order	My weekly words using magazine letters

Directions: Pick a circle. Circle it. Color in the circle when you are done.

My weekly words

Words and pictures

All of my weekly words

Directions: Pick a diamond. Circle it. Color in the diamond when you are done.

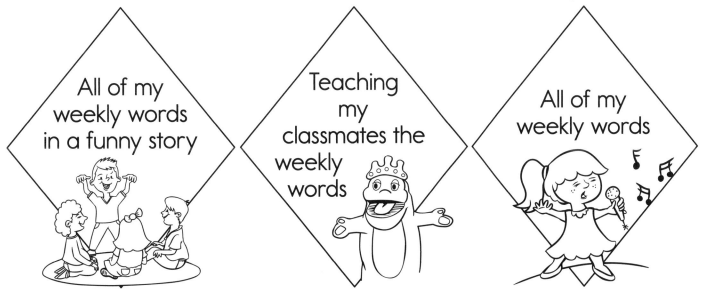

All of my weekly words in a funny story

Teaching my classmates the weekly words

All of my weekly words

SPELLING

Directions: Pick a square. Circle it. Color in the square when you are done.

Create a set of **concentration cards** for your weekly words. 	Design a **windowpane** for your weekly words. Be creative with your drawings! 	Using letters from a magazine, make a **collage** of your weekly words. 

Directions: Pick a circle. Circle it. Color in the circle when you are done.

Make an **acrostic** for 2 of your weekly words.

Write the word
Oval letters
Remember the word
Draw a picture

Using all of your weekly words, create a **crossword puzzle**. Do not always use the definition for the clue!

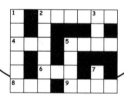

Create a **mind map** for your weekly words to show how they are related to each other.

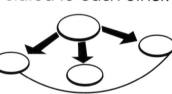

✂ -

Directions: Pick a diamond. Circle it. Color in the diamond when you are done.

Using recycled materials, create a spelling **puppet** to help your classmates remember the weekly words.

Make a weekly word **board game** to help your classmates practice all of the weekly words.

Create a **song** that has all of your weekly words in it. Be sure your song uses the words—don't just list them!

PARTS OF SPEECH

THREE-SHAPE MENU ● AND TIC-TAC-TOE MENU ▲

Reading and Communication Objectives Covered Through This Menu and These Activities

- Students will determine meanings of words and develop vocabulary.
- Students will identify nouns and verbs.
- Students will use reference materials to build word meanings.

Writing Objectives Covered Through This Menu and These Activities

- Students will write to record their ideas and reflections.
- Students will record their knowledge in a variety of ways.
- Students will write to express their feelings or to reflect.
- Students will write to inform, explain, describe, or narrate.

Materials Needed by Students for Completion

- Blank index cards (for trading cards and mobiles)
- Coat hangers (for mobiles)
- String (for mobiles)
- Magazines (for collages)
- Verb Cube template
- Scrapbooking materials

Special Notes on the Modifications of These Menus

- This topic has two different menu formats: the Three-Shape menu ▲ and the Tic-Tac-Toe menu ●. The Three-Shape menu is specifically selected for the lower level option as it easily allows the menu to be broken into manageable bits. The menu itself can be cut along the dotted lines into strips of the same shape. Students can then be given the strip of square product choices for their use. Once they have chosen and submitted that product for grading, they can be given the circle strip, and finally the diamond strip. Because this type of menu is designed to become more advanced as students move through the shapes, teachers may choose to provide their lower level students with just the top two shapes and save the diamonds for enrichment.

Special Notes on the Use of These Menus

- The lower level menu ▲ is specifically designed for students who are lower level readers or for those with a more limited vocabulary. It is meant to simply remind students of product options that have already been explained.

Time Frame

- 1–2 weeks—Students are given a menu as the unit is started. As the teacher presents lessons throughout the week, he or she should refer back to the menu options associated with that content. The teacher will go over all of the options for that content and have students select the activities they are most interested in completing. As teaching continues over the next week, activities are completed. For those students working on the Tic-Tac-Toe menu ●, the selected activities should make a column or row. The teacher may choose to dedicate a learning center to working on menu products or simply allow students time to work after other work is finished. When students complete this pattern, they will have completed one activity from each content area, learning style, or level of Bloom's revised taxonomy, depending on the design of the menu.
- 1 week—At the start of the unit, the teacher chooses the three activities he or she feels are most valuable for students. Stations can be set up in the classroom. These three activities are available for student choice throughout the week as regular instruction takes place.
- 1–2 days—The teacher chooses an activity from the menu to use with the entire class.

Suggested Forms

- All-purpose rubric

Name:_____ ▲

PARTS OF SPEECH

Directions: Pick a square. Circle it. Color in the square when you are done.

My 8 favorite nouns	Examples of the different types of nouns	8 nouns from my classroom
	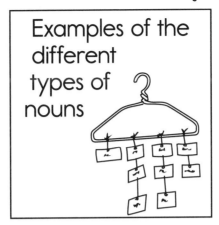	

✂ -

Directions: Pick a circle. Circle it. Color in the circle when you are done.

Verbs or activities	My favorite verbs	8 verbs with a sentence for each

✂ -

Directions: Pick a diamond. Circle it. Color in the diamond when you are done.

Adjectives that describe me	For someone in my family	Something that is special to me

Name:_____

PARTS OF SPEECH

Directions: Check the boxes you plan to complete. They should form a tic-tac-toe across or down. All activities must be completed by _____.

☐ **People, Places, and Things** Create a set of **trading cards** for your favorite 10 nouns. 	☐ **Describing Words** Perform a **skit** about adjectives that describe your daily life. 	☐ **Action Words** Make a **list** of verbs. Include a sentence using each one. 
☐ **Action Words** Create a **cube** with pictures and information about the verbs or activities you enjoy most. 	☐ **People, Places, and Things** Design a **mobile** to show examples of the different types of nouns. 	☐ **Describing Words** Make a **greeting card** for a member of your family. Describe what about that person makes him or her deserve the card.
☐ **Describing Words** Design a **collage** with adjectives that describe you. 	☐ **Action Words** Make a **scrapbook** about yourself and your favorite verbs. 	☐ **People, Places, and Things** Create a **class game** to help your classmates practice giving examples of the different types of nouns.

VERB CUBE

Directions: Rank the activities or verbs you enjoy doing the most on this **cube**. Draw pictures and write about these activities or verbs in order, with your favorite listed first and your least favorite last. Use this pattern or create your own cube.

Number 1
Activity/Verb

Number 2
Activity/Verb

Number 3
Activity/Verb

Number 4
Activity/Verb

Number 5
Activity/Verb

Number 6
Activity/Verb

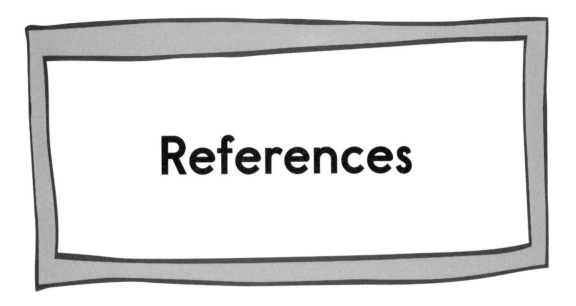

References

Anderson, L. W., & Krathwohl, D. R. (Eds.). (2001). *A taxonomy for learning, teaching, and assessing: A revision of Bloom's taxonomy of educational objectives.* New York, NY: Allyn & Bacon.

Cipani, E. (1995). Inclusive education: What do we know and what do we still have to learn? *Exceptional Children, 61,* 498–500.

Cusumano, C., & Mueller, J. (2007). How differentiated instruction helps struggling students. *Educational Leadership, 36*(4), 8–10

Mercer, C. D., Lane, H. B., Jordan, L., Allsopp, D. H., & Eisele, M. R. (1996). Empowering teachers and students with instructional choices in inclusive settings. *Remedial and Special Education, 17,* 226–236.

Shevin, M., & Klein, N. (2004). The importance of choice-making skills for students with severe disabilities. *Research & Practice for Persons With Severe Disabilities, 29,* 161–168.

Note

The articles by Cipani (1995), Cusumano and Mueller (2007), and Shevin and Klein (2004) were used to gather background information on inclusion, differentiated instruction, and choice for this book.

Appendix: Book Lists

CALDECOTT MEDAL WINNERS (THROUGH 2012)

2012: *A Ball for Daisy* by Chris Raschka

2011: *A Sick Day for Amos McGee* illustrated by Erin E. Stead and written by Philip C. Stead

2010: *The Lion & the Mouse* by Jerry Pinkney

2009: *The House in the Night* illustrated by Beth Krommes and written by Susan Marie Swanson

2008: *The Invention of Hugo Cabret* by Brian Selznick

2007: *Flotsam* by David Wiesner

2006: *The Hello, Goodbye Window* illustrated by Chris Raschka and written by Norton Juster

2005: *Kitten's First Full Moon* by Kevin Henkes

2004: *The Man Who Walked Between the Towers* by Mordicai Gerstein

2003: *My Friend Rabbit* by Eric Rohmann

2002: *The Three Pigs* by David Wiesner

2001: *So You Want to Be President?* illustrated by David Small and written by Judith St. George

2000: *Joseph Had a Little Overcoat* by Simms Taback

1999: *Snowflake Bentley* illustrated by Mary Azarian and written by Jacqueline Briggs Martin

1998: *Rapunzel* by Paul O. Zelinsky

1997: *Golem* by David Wisniewski

1996: *Officer Buckle and Gloria* by Peggy Rathmann

1995: *Smoky Night* illustrated by David Diaz and written by Eve Bunting

1994: *Grandfather's Journey* by Allen Say

1993: *Mirette on the High Wire* by Emily Arnold McCully

1992: *Tuesday* by David Wiesner

1991: *Black and White* by David Macaulay

1990: *Lon Po Po: A Red-Riding Hood Story From China* by Ed Young

1989: *Song and Dance Man* illustrated by Stephen Gammell and written by Karen Ackerman

1988: *Owl Moon* illustrated by John Schoenherr and written by Jane Yolen

1987: *Hey, Al* illustrated by Richard Egielski and written by Arthur Yorinks

1986: *The Polar Express* by Chris Van Allsburg

1985: *Saint George and the Dragon* illustrated by Trina Schart Hyman and retold by Margaret Hodges

1984: *The Glorious Flight: Across the Channel With Louis Bleriot* by Alice and Martin Provensen

1983: *Shadow* translated and illustrated by Marcia Brown

1982: *Jumanji* by Chris Van Allsburg

1981: *Fables* by Arnold Lobel

1980: *Ox-Cart Man* illustrated by Barbara Cooney and written by Donald Hall

1979: *The Girl Who Loved Wild Horses* by Paul Goble

1978: *Noah's Ark* by Peter Spier

1977: *Ashanti to Zulu: African Traditions* illustrated by Leo and Diane Dillon and written by Margaret Musgrove

1976: *Why Mosquitoes Buzz in People's Ears: A West African Tale* illustrated by Leo and Diane Dillon and retold by Verna Aardema

1975: *Arrow to the Sun* by Gerald McDermott

1974: *Duffy and the Devil* illustrated by Margot Zemach and retold by Harve Zemach

1973: *The Funny Little Woman* illustrated by Blair Lent and retold by Arlene Mosel

1972: *One Fine Day* illustrated and retold by Nonny Hogrogian

1971: *A Story A Story* illustrated and retold by Gail E. Haley

1970: *Sylvester and the Magic Pebble* by William Steig

1969: *The Fool of the World and the Flying Ship: A Russian Tale* illustrated by Uri Shulevitz and retold by Arthur Ransome

1968: *Drummer Hoff* illustrated by Ed Emberley and adapted by Barbara Emberley

1967: *Sam, Bangs & Moonshine* by Evaline Ness

1966: *Always Room for One More* illustrated by Nonny Hogrogian and written by Sorche Nic Leodhas

1965: *May I Bring a Friend?* illustrated by Beni Montresor and written by Beatrice Schenk de Regniers

1964: *Where the Wild Things Are* by Maurice Sendak

1963: *The Snowy Day* by Ezra Jack Keats

1962: *Once a Mouse . . .* illustrated and retold by Marcia Brown

1961: *Baboushka and the Three Kings* illustrated by Nicolas Sidjakov and written by Ruth Robbins

1960: *Nine Days to Christmas: A Story of Mexico* illustrated by Marie Hall Ets and written by Marie Hall Ets and Aurora Labastida

1959: *Chanticleer and the Fox* illustrated and adapted by Barbara Cooney

1958: *Time of Wonder* by Robert McCloskey

1957: *A Tree Is Nice* illustrated by Marc Simont and written by Janice May Udry

1956: *Frog Went A-Courtin'* illustrated by Feodor Rojankovsky and retold by John Langstaff

1955: *Cinderella, or the Little Glass Slipper* illustrated and translated by Marcia Brown

1954: *Madeline's Rescue* by Ludwig Bemelmans

1953: *The Biggest Bear* by Lynd Ward

1952: *Finders Keepers* illustrated by Nicholas Mordvinoff and written by William Lipkind

1951: *The Egg Tree* by Katherine Milhous

1950: *Song of the Swallows* by Leo Politi

1949: *The Big Snow* by Berta and Elmer Hader

1948: *White Snow, Bright Snow* illustrated by Roger Duvoisin and written by Alvin Tresselt

1947: *The Little Island* illustrated by Leonard Weisgard and written by Margaret Wise Brown

1946: *The Rooster Crows* by Maud and Miska Petersham

1945: *Prayer for a Child* illustrated by Elizabeth Orton Jones and written by Rachel Field

1944: *Many Moons* illustrated by Louis Slobodkin and written by James Thurber

1943: *The Little House* by Virginia Lee Burton

1942: *Make Way for Ducklings* by Robert McCloskey

1941: *They Were Strong and Good* by Robert Lawson

1940: *Abraham Lincoln* by Ingri and Edgar Parin d'Aulaire

1939: *Mei Li* by Thomas Handforth

1938: *Animals of the Bible: A Picture Book* illustrated by Dorothy P. Lathrop and text selected by Helen Dean Fish

ALPHABET BOOKS

Mouse Letters: A Very First Alphabet Book by Jim Arnosky

Black and White Rabbit's ABC by Alan Baker

The Animal ABC by Leslie A. Baker

Girls: A to Z by Eve Bunting

ABC I Like Me! by Nancy L. Carlson

The Hullabaloo ABC by Beverly Cleary

Firefighters A to Z by Chris L. Demarest

G Is for One Gzonk! An Alpha-Number-Bet Book by Tony DiTerlizzi

Dog's ABC: A Silly Story About the Alphabet by Emma Dodd

Eating the Alphabet: Fruits and Vegetables From A to Z by Lois Ehlert

The Turn-Around, Upside-Down Alphabet Book by Lisa Campbell Ernst

Kipper's A to Z: An Alphabet Adventure by Mick Inkpen

On Your Toes: A Ballet ABC by Rachel Isadora

ABC: A Child's First Alphabet Book by Alison Jay

Miss Spider's ABC by David Kirk

K Is for Kitten by Nick Clark Leopold

A Is for Salad by Mike Lester

Chicka Chicka Boom Boom by Bill Martin, Jr. & John Archambault

I Spy: An Alphabet in Art by Lucy Micklethwait

My "a" Book by Jane Belk Moncure

ABCD: An Alphabet Book of Cats and Dogs by Shelia Moxley

The Beetle Alphabet Book by Jerry Pallotta

The Handmade Alphabet by Laura Rankin

A Big and Little Alphabet by Liz Rosenberg

The Hidden Alphabet by Laura Vaccaro Seeger

On Beyond Zebra! by Dr. Seuss

The Z Was Zapped: A Play in Twenty-Six Acts by Chris Van Allsburg

Alphabet Mystery by Audrey Wood

FOLK TALE AND FAIRY TALE BOOKS

The Dragon New Year: A Chinese Legend by David Bouchard

The Egyptian Cinderella by Shirley Climo

The Willow Maiden by Gal Collins

The Terrible EEK: A Japanese Tale by Patricia A. Compton

Stella, Fairy of the Forest by Marie-Louise Gay

Anansi by Brian Gleeson

Princess Furball by Charlotte Huck

Baba Yaga: A Russian Folktale by Eric A. Kimmel

John Henry by Julius Lester

Stories From Arabian Nights by Naomi Lewis

Cinderella by Michele Marineau

The Paper Bag Princess by Robert N. Munsch

The Little Flower King by Kvĕta Pacovská

The Love of Two Stars: A Korean Legend by Janie Jaehyun Park

Petrosinella: A Neapolitan Rapunzel by Diane Stanley

Mufaro's Beautiful Daughters: An African Tale by John Steptoe

Little Water and the Gift of the Animals: A Seneca Legend by C. J. Taylor

The Woodcutter's Duck by Krystyna Turska

The Emperor and the Kite by Jane Yolen

Sleeping Ugly by Jane Yolen

Rapunzel by Paul O. Zelinsky

About the Author

After teaching science for more than 15 years, both overseas and in the U.S., **Laurie E. Westphal** now works as an independent gifted education and science consultant nationwide. She enjoys developing and presenting staff development on differentiation for various districts and conferences, working with teachers to assist them in planning and developing lessons to meet the needs of all students. Laurie currently resides in Houston, TX, and has made it her goal to convert as many teachers as she can to the differentiated lifestyle in the classroom and share her vision for real-world, product-based lessons that help all students become critical thinkers and effective problem solvers.

If you are interested in having Laurie speak at your next staff development day or conference, please visit her website, http://www.giftedconsultant.com, for additional information.

Additional Titles by the Author

Laurie E. Westphal has written many books on using differentiation strategies in the classroom, providing teachers of grades K–8 with creative, engaging, ready-to-use resources. Among them are:

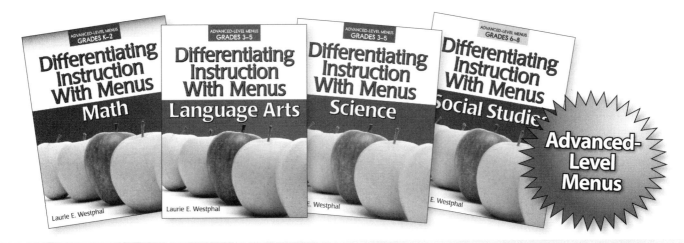

Differentiating Instruction With Menus, Grades K–2
(Math, Language Arts, Science, and Social Studies volumes available)

Differentiating Instruction With Menus, Grades 3–5
(Math, Language Arts, Science, and Social Studies volumes available)

Differentiating Instruction With Menus, Grades 6–8
(Math, Language Arts, Science, and Social Studies volumes available)

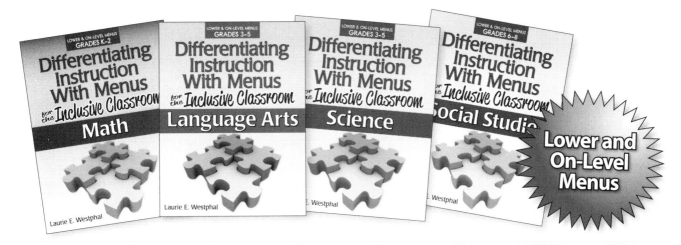

Differentiating Instruction With Menus for the Inclusive Classroom, Grades K–2
(Math, Language Arts, Science, and Social Studies volumes available)

Differentiating Instruction With Menus for the Inclusive Classroom, Grades 3–5
(Math, Language Arts, Science, and Social Studies volumes available)

Differentiating Instruction With Menus for the Inclusive Classroom, Grades 6–8
(Math, Language Arts, Science, and Social Studies volumes available)

**For a current listing of Laurie's books, please visit
Prufrock Press at http://www.prufrock.com.**